# FAVORITE BRAND NAME™
# CAKE MIX

Publications International, Ltd.

Favorite Brand Name Recipes at www.fbnr.com

**Pictured on the front cover** *(clockwise from top left):* Chocolate Sweetheart Cupcakes *(page 326),* Flower Power Strawberry Cake *(page 248),* Pastel Mint Swirls *(page 140),* Cookies 'n' Cream Cake *(page 12),* Chocolate Glazed Citrus Poppy Seed Cake *(page 6)* and Chocolate and Oat Toffee Bars *(page 170).*
**Pictured on the back jacket flap:** Mango-Orange Pound Cake *(page 272).*
**Pictured on the back cover** *(clockwise from top):* Chocolate Peanut Butter Candy Bars *(page 312),* Whoopie Pies *(page 142),* Chocolate-Covered Coconut Almond Cake *(page 46)* and Boston Cream Cupcakes *(page 74).*

ISBN-13: 978-1-4127-9676-7
ISBN-10: 1-4127-9676-8

Library of Congress Control Number: 2008924407

Manufactured in China.

8 7 6 5 4 3 2 1

**Microwave Cooking:** Microwave ovens vary in wattage. Use the cooking times as guidelines and check for doneness before adding more time.
**Preparation/Cooking Times:** Preparation times are based on the approximate amount of time required to assemble the recipe before cooking, baking, chilling or serving. These times include preparation steps such as measuring, chopping and mixing. The fact that some preparations and cooking can be done simultaneously is taken into account. Preparation of optional ingredients and serving suggestions is not included.

# Table of Contents

# Cake Mix

## *Classics*

# chocolate glazed citrus poppy seed cake

1 package (about 18 ounces) lemon cake mix
1 container (8 ounces) plain lowfat yogurt
3 eggs
⅓ cup milk
⅓ cup poppy seeds
1 teaspoon freshly grated lemon peel
   Chocolate Citrus Glaze (recipe follows)

1. Heat oven to 350°F. Grease and flour 12-cup fluted tube pan or 10-inch tube pan.

2. Combine cake mix, yogurt, eggs, milk, poppy seeds and lemon peel in large bowl; beat until well blended. Pour batter into prepared pan.

3. Bake 40 to 45 minutes or until wooden pick inserted in center comes out clean. Cool 20 minutes; remove from pan to wire rack. Cool completely.

4. Prepare Chocolate Citrus Glaze; spoon over cake, allowing glaze to run down sides.                              *Makes 12 servings*

Chocolate Citrus Glaze: Melt 2 tablespoons butter or margarine in small saucepan over medium heat. Stir in 2 tablespoons HERSHEY'S Cocoa or HERSHEY'S SPECIAL DARK™ Cocoa, 2 tablespoons water, 1 tablespoon orange-flavored liqueur, if desired, and ½ teaspoon orange extract. Whisk in 1¼ cups powdered sugar until smooth. If glaze is too thin, whisk in additional ¼ cup powdered sugar. Use immediately.

# easy upside down cake

1 can (20 ounces) DOLE® Pineapple Slices
¼ cup butter or margarine, melted
⅔ cup packed brown sugar
10 maraschino cherries
1 package (18.25 ounces) yellow or pineapple-flavored cake mix

• Drain pineapple, reserving ¾ cup juice.

• Stir together melted butter and brown sugar in 12-inch skillet with heatproof handle. Arrange pineapple slices in sugar mixture. Place cherry in center of each pineapple slice.

• Prepare cake mix according to package directions, replacing water with reserved ¾ cup juice. Pour batter evenly over pineapple.

• Bake at 350°F 40 to 45 minutes or until toothpick inserted in center comes out clean.

• Cool 5 minutes. Loosen edges and invert onto serving platter.

*Makes 10 servings*

Note: Cake can be baked in 13×9-inch baking pan instead of skillet. Prepare and assemble cake as above except cut two pineapple slices in half and place whole slices along edges of pan and halved slices in center. Place cherries in center of slices. Bake and cool as above.

Mini Upside Down Cakes: **Drain** 1 can (20 ounces) DOLE® Crushed Pineapple, reserving juice. Grease 24 muffin cups. **Stir** ⅓ cup melted butter with ⅔ cup packed brown sugar. Evenly spoon mixture into bottoms of cups; spoon about 1 tablespoon crushed pineapple over sugar mixture. **Prepare** cake mix as above. Evenly pour batter into cups. **Bake** 20 to 25 minutes. Invert onto serving platter. Makes 24 servings.

Prep Time: **15 minutes**
Bake Time: **40 minutes**

# pink lady cake

1 package (about 18 ounces) devil's food cake mix, plus ingredients
   to prepare mix
1 container (16 ounces) vanilla frosting
   Red food coloring
1 package (3 ounces) ladyfingers, split in half

1. Preheat oven to 350°F. Grease two 8-inch round cake pans.

2. Prepare cake mix according to package directions. Spread batter evenly in prepared pans.

3. Bake 30 minutes or until toothpick inserted into centers comes out clean. Cool cake layers completely in pans on wire racks.

4. Blend frosting and food coloring in medium bowl until desired shade of pink is reached. Remove cake layers from pans. Place one layer on serving plate; spread with ½ cup frosting. Top with second cake layer; frost top and side of cake with remaining frosting.

5. Arrange ladyfingers around side of cake, pressing flat sides into frosting as shown in photo. Tie ribbon around cake, if desired.

*Makes 12 servings*

# banana fudge layer cake

1 package DUNCAN HINES® Moist Deluxe® Yellow Cake Mix
1⅓ cups water
3 eggs
⅓ cup vegetable oil
1 cup mashed ripe bananas (about 3 medium)
1 container DUNCAN HINES® Chocolate Frosting

1. Preheat oven to 350°F. Grease and flour two 9-inch round cake pans.

2. Combine cake mix, water, eggs and oil in large bowl. Beat at low speed with electric mixer until moistened. Beat at medium speed 2 minutes. Stir in bananas.

3. Pour into prepared pans. Bake at 350°F for 28 to 31 minutes or until toothpick inserted in center comes out clean. Cool in pans 15 minutes. Remove from pans; cool completely.

4. Fill and frost cake with frosting. Garnish as desired.

*Makes 12 to 16 servings*

To ripen bananas, store them at room temperature. To speed ripening, place them in an unsealed paper bag. Brown speckles on the skins are an indication of ripeness, and black patches means the bananas are overripe. (Overripe bananas are still good to use in baking.)

# cookies 'n' cream cake

1 package (about 18 ounces) white cake mix *without* pudding
    in the mix
1 package (4-serving size) white chocolate instant pudding
    and pie filling mix
1 cup vegetable oil
4 egg whites
½ cup milk
20 chocolate sandwich cookies, coarsely chopped
½ cup semisweet chocolate chips
1 teaspoon shortening
4 chocolate sandwich cookies, cut into quarters

1. Preheat oven to 350°F. Spray 12-cup bundt pan with nonstick cooking spray.

2. Beat cake mix, pudding mix, oil, egg whites and milk in large bowl with electric mixer at medium speed 2 minutes or until ingredients are well blended. Stir in chopped cookies. Spread batter in prepared pan.

3. Bake 50 to 60 minutes or until cake springs back when lightly touched. Cool cake in pan 1 hour. Invert onto wire rack; cool completely.

4. Combine chocolate chips and shortening in small microwavable bowl. Microwave on HIGH 1 minute; stir. Microwave at 15-second intervals, as necessary, stirring until melted and smooth. Drizzle glaze over cake and garnish with quartered cookies.                    *Makes 12 servings*

# elegant chocolate angel torte

⅓ cup HERSHEY'S Cocoa
1 package (about 16 ounces) angel food cake mix
2 envelopes (1.3 ounces each) dry whipped topping mix
1 cup cold nonfat milk
1 teaspoon vanilla extract
1 cup strawberry purée*
   Strawberries

*Mash 2 cups sliced fresh strawberries (or frozen berries, thawed) in blender or food processor. Cover; blend until smooth. Purée should measure 1 cup.

1. Move oven rack to lowest position.

2. Sift cocoa over dry cake mix in large bowl; stir to blend. Proceed with mixing cake as directed on package. Bake and cool as directed for 10-inch tube pan. Carefully run knife along side of pan to loosen cake; remove from pan. Using serrated knife, slice cake horizontally into four layers.

3. Prepare whipped topping mix as directed on package, using 1 cup nonfat milk and 1 teaspoon vanilla. Fold in strawberry purée.

4. Place bottom cake layer on serving plate; spread with ¼ of strawberry topping. Set next cake layer on top; spread with ¼ of topping. Continue layering cake and topping. Garnish with strawberries. Refrigerate until ready to serve. Slice cake with sharp serrated knife, cutting with gentle sawing motion. Cover; refrigerate leftover cake.         *Makes about 16 servings*

Prep Time: 30 minutes
Bake Time: 45 minutes
Cool Time: 2 hours

# coconut lemon torte

1 (14-ounce) can EAGLE BRAND® Sweetened Condensed Milk
   (NOT evaporated milk)
2 egg yolks
½ cup lemon juice
1 teaspoon grated lemon rind (optional)
   Yellow food coloring (optional)
1 (18.25- or 18.5-ounce) package white cake mix
1 (4-ounce) container frozen nondairy whipped topping, thawed
   (1¾ cups)
   Flaked coconut

1. In medium saucepan, combine EAGLE BRAND®, egg yolks, lemon juice, lemon rind (optional) and food coloring (optional). Over medium heat, cook and stir until slightly thickened, about 10 minutes. Chill.

2. Preheat oven to 350°F. Grease and flour two 9-inch round cake pans. Prepare cake mix as package directs. Pour batter into prepared pans. Bake 30 minutes or until lightly browned. Remove from pans; cool completely.

3. With sharp knife, remove crust from top of each cake layer. Split layers horizontally. Spread equal portions of lemon mixture between layers and on top to within 1 inch of edge.

4. Frost side and 1-inch rim on top of cake with whipped topping. Coat side of cake with coconut; garnish as desired. Store leftovers covered in refrigerator.                          *Makes one (9-inch) cake*

# delicate white chocolate cake

1 package DUNCAN HINES® Moist Deluxe® White Cake Mix
1 package (4-serving size) vanilla-flavor instant pudding and
    pie filling mix
4 egg whites
1 cup water
½ cup vegetable oil
5 ounces finely chopped white chocolate
1 cup cherry preserves
8 drops red food coloring (optional)
2 cups whipping cream, chilled
2 tablespoons confectioners' sugar
    Maraschino cherries for garnish
1 ounce white chocolate shavings for garnish

1. Preheat oven to 350°F. Cut waxed paper circles to fit bottoms of three 9-inch round cake pans. Grease bottoms and sides of pans. Line with waxed paper circles.

2. Combine cake mix, pudding mix, egg whites, water and oil in large mixing bowl. Beat at medium speed with electric mixer for 2 minutes. Fold in chopped white chocolate. Pour into prepared pans. Bake at 350°F for 18 to 22 minutes or until toothpick inserted in center comes out clean. Cool in pans 15 minutes. Invert onto cooling racks. Peel off waxed paper. Cool completely.

3. Combine cherry preserves and food coloring, if desired. Stir to blend color.

4. Beat whipping cream in large bowl until soft peaks form. Add sugar gradually. Beat until stiff peaks form.

*continued on page 20*

5. To assemble, place one cake layer on serving plate. Spread ½ cup cherry preserves over cake. Place second cake layer on top. Spread with remaining preserves. Place third cake layer on top. Frost side and top of cake with whipped cream. Decorate with maraschino cherries and white chocolate shavings. Refrigerate until ready to serve.

*Makes 12 to 16 servings*

# butterscotch bundt cake

- **1 package (about 18 ounces) yellow cake mix *without* pudding in the mix**
- **1 package (4-serving size) butterscotch instant pudding and pie filling mix**
- **1 cup water**
- **3 eggs**
- **2 teaspoons ground cinnamon**
- **½ cup chopped pecans**
- **Powdered sugar**

1. Preheat oven to 325°F. Spray 12-cup bundt pan with nonstick cooking spray.

2. Beat cake mix, pudding mix, water, eggs and cinnamon in large bowl with electric mixer at medium-high speed 2 minutes or until blended. Stir in pecans. Pour batter into prepared pan.

3. Bake 40 to 50 minutes or until cake springs back when lightly touched. Cool in pan on wire rack 10 minutes. Invert cake onto wire rack; cool completely. Sprinkle with powdered sugar.　　*Makes 12 to 16 servings*

Pistachio Walnut Bundt Cake: Substitute white cake mix for yellow cake mix, pistachio pudding mix for butterscotch pudding mix and walnuts for pecans.

# candy bar cake

1 package (about 18 ounces) devil's food cake mix *without* pudding in the mix
1 cup sour cream
4 eggs
$\frac{1}{3}$ cup vegetable oil
$\frac{1}{4}$ cup water
3 containers (16 ounces each) white frosting
1 bar (2.1 ounces) chocolate-covered crispy peanut butter candy, chopped
1 bar (2.07 ounces) chocolate-covered peanut, caramel and nougat candy, chopped
1 bar (1.4 ounces) chocolate-covered toffee candy, chopped
4 bars (1.55 ounces each) milk chocolate

1. Preheat oven to 350°F. Grease and flour two 9-inch round cake pans.

2. Beat cake mix, sour cream, eggs, oil and water in large bowl with electric mixer at low speed 1 minute or until blended. Increase speed to medium; beat 1 to 2 minutes or until smooth. Spread batter in prepared pans.

3. Bake 30 to 35 minutes or until toothpick inserted into centers comes out clean. Cool cake layers in pans 10 minutes. Remove from pans; cool completely on wire racks.

4. Cut each cake layer in half horizontally. Place one cake layer on serving plate. Spread generously with frosting. Sprinkle with one chopped candy bar. Repeat with two more cake layers, additional frosting and remaining two chopped candy bars. Top with remaining cake layer; frost top of cake with remaining frosting.

5. Break milk chocolate bars into pieces along score lines. Stand chocolate pieces in frosting around outside edge of cake.          *Makes 12 servings*

# almond cake

1 can (8 ounces) almond paste
3 eggs
1 package (about 18 ounces) white cake mix
1¼ cups water
⅓ cup vegetable oil
1 cup seedless raspberry preserves
1 container (12 ounces) whipped vanilla frosting
    Candy-coated almonds

1. Preheat oven to 350°F. Grease two 9-inch round cake pans.

2. Combine almond paste and eggs in large bowl; stir until completely smooth. Add cake mix, water and oil; beat with electric mixer at low speed 1 minute. Beat at medium-low speed 2 minutes or until well blended. Pour batter into prepared pans.

3. Bake 35 minutes or until toothpick inserted into centers comes out clean. Cool completely in pans on wire racks.

4. Remove cake layers from pans. Place one layer on serving plate; spread with preserves to within ¼ inch of edge. Top with remaining cake layer. Frost top and side of cake with frosting. Decorate with almonds.

*Makes 12 servings*

# carrot layer cake

**Cake**

    1 package DUNCAN HINES® Moist Deluxe® Classic Yellow Cake Mix

    4 eggs

    ½ cup vegetable oil

    3 cups grated carrots

    1 cup finely chopped nuts

    2 teaspoons ground cinnamon

**Cream Cheese Frosting**

    1 package (8 ounces) cream cheese, softened

    ¼ cup (½ stick) butter or margarine, softened

    2 teaspoons vanilla extract

    4 cups confectioners' sugar

**1.** Preheat oven to 350°F. Grease and flour two 8- or 9-inch round baking pans.

**2.** For cake, combine cake mix, eggs, oil, carrots, nuts and cinnamon in large bowl. Beat at low speed with electric mixer until moistened. Beat at medium speed for 2 minutes. Pour into prepared pans. Bake at 350°F for 35 to 40 minutes or until toothpick inserted into centers comes out clean. Cool.

**3.** For cream cheese frosting, place cream cheese, butter and vanilla extract in large bowl. Beat at low speed until smooth and creamy. Add confectioners' sugar gradually, beating until smooth. Add more sugar to thicken, or milk or water to thin frosting, as needed. Fill and frost cooled cake. Garnish with whole pecans. *Makes 12 to 16 servings*

# german upside-down cake

1½ cups shredded coconut
1 cup pecan pieces
1 container (16 ounces) coconut pecan frosting
1 package (about 18 ounces) German chocolate cake mix
1⅓ cups water
4 eggs
1 cup milk chocolate chips
⅓ cup vegetable oil
Whipped cream (optional)

**1.** Preheat oven to 350°F. Spray 13×9-inch glass baking dish with nonstick cooking spray.

**2.** Spread coconut evenly in prepared pan. Sprinkle pecans over coconut. Spoon frosting by tablespoonfuls over pecans. (Do not spread.)

**3.** Beat cake mix, water, eggs, chocolate chips and oil in large bowl with electric mixer at low speed 30 seconds. Beat at medium speed 2 minutes or until well blended and creamy. Pour batter into prepared pan, spreading carefully over frosting.

**4.** Bake 35 to 40 minutes or until toothpick inserted into center comes out clean. Cool in pan 10 minutes; invert onto serving plate. Serve warm; top with whipped cream, if desired. *Makes 16 to 18 servings*

# fudgy ripple cake

1 package (18.25 ounces) yellow cake mix, plus ingredients
    to prepare mix
1 package (3 ounces) cream cheese, softened
2 tablespoons unsweetened cocoa powder
    Fudgy Glaze (recipe follows)
½ cup "M&M's"® Chocolate Mini Baking Bits

Preheat oven to 350°F. Lightly grease and flour 10-inch bundt or ring pan; set aside. Prepare cake mix as package directs. In medium bowl combine 1½ cups prepared batter, cream cheese and cocoa powder until smooth. Pour half of yellow batter into prepared pan. Drop spoonfuls of chocolate batter over yellow batter in pan. Top with remaining yellow batter. Bake about 45 minutes or until toothpick inserted near center comes out clean. Cool completely on wire rack. Unmold cake onto serving plate. Prepare Fudgy Glaze; spread over top of cake, allowing some glaze to run over side. Sprinkle with "M&M's"® Chocolate Mini Baking Bits. Store in tightly covered container.                                    *Makes 10 servings*

Fudgy Glaze: Place 1 square (1 ounce) semi-sweet chocolate in small microwave-safe bowl. Microwave at HIGH 30 seconds; stir. Repeat as necessary until chocolate is completely melted, stirring at 10-second intervals; set aside. In medium bowl combine 1 cup powdered sugar and ⅓ cup unsweetened cocoa powder. Stir in 3 tablespoons milk, ½ teaspoon vanilla extract and melted chocolate until smooth.

# red velvet cake

2 packages (about 18 ounces each) white cake mix
2 teaspoons baking soda
3 cups buttermilk
4 eggs
2 bottles (1 ounce each) red food coloring
2 containers (16 ounces each) vanilla frosting

1. Preheat oven to 350°F. Grease and flour four 9-inch round cake pans.

2. Combine cake mixes and baking soda in large bowl. Add buttermilk, eggs and food coloring; beat with electric mixer at low speed until moistened. Beat at high speed 2 minutes. Pour batter into prepared pans.

3. Bake 30 to 35 minutes or until toothpick inserted into centers comes out clean. Cool cake layers in pans 10 minutes. Remove from pans; cool completely on wire racks.

4. Place one cake layer on serving plate; spread with frosting. Repeat with second and third cake layers. Top with fourth cake layer; frost top and side of cake.

*Makes 16 servings*

# boston cream pie

1 package DUNCAN HINES® Moist Deluxe® Classic Yellow Cake Mix
2 containers (3½ ounces each) ready-to-eat vanilla pudding
1 container DUNCAN HINES® Chocolate Frosting

1. Preheat oven to 350°F. Grease and flour two 8- or 9-inch round pans.

2. Prepare, bake and cool cakes following package directions for basic recipe.

3. To assemble, place one cake layer on serving plate. Spread contents of 2 containers of vanilla pudding on top of cake. Top with second cake layer. Remove lid and foil top of Chocolate frosting container. Heat in microwave oven at HIGH (100% power) for 25 to 30 seconds. Stir. (Mixture should be thin.) Spread chocolate glaze over top of second cake layer. Refrigerate until ready to serve.           *Makes 12 to 16 servings*

For a richer flavor, substitute DUNCAN HINES® Butter Recipe Golden Cake Mix in place of Yellow Cake Mix.

# pecan praline brandy cake

1 package (about 18 ounces) butter pecan cake mix
¾ cup water
⅓ cup plain yogurt
2 egg whites
1 egg
¼ cup plus ½ teaspoon brandy, divided
2 tablespoons vegetable oil
1 cup chopped toasted pecans, divided
⅔ cup packed light brown sugar
⅓ cup light corn syrup
¼ cup whipping cream
2 tablespoons butter
½ teaspoon vanilla

1. Preheat oven to 350°F. Spray 10- or 12-cup bundt pan with nonstick cooking spray.

2. Beat cake mix, water, yogurt, egg whites, egg, ¼ cup brandy and oil in large bowl with electric mixer at low speed 30 seconds. Beat at medium speed 2 minutes or until light and fluffy. Fold in ½ cup pecans. Pour batter into prepared pan.

3. Bake 50 to 60 minutes or until toothpick inserted near center comes out clean. Cool cake in pan 10 minutes. Invert onto wire rack; cool completely.

4. Combine brown sugar, corn syrup, cream and butter in small saucepan. Bring to a boil over medium heat, stirring constantly. Remove from heat; stir in remaining ½ cup pecans, ½ teaspoon brandy and vanilla. Cool to room temperature (glaze should be thick but still pourable). Pour glaze over top of cake. Serve immediately or store covered at room temperature until ready to serve. *Makes 12 servings*

# toasted almond supreme

1 package (about 18 ounces) devil's food cake mix, plus ingredients to prepare mix

1¼ cups strong coffee

2 cups cold whipping cream

¾ cup powdered sugar

2 tablespoons unsweetened cocoa powder

1½ teaspoons vanilla

½ cup seedless red raspberry jam

1 cup sliced almonds, toasted*

Fresh raspberries (optional)

*To toast almonds, spread in single layer on baking sheet. Bake in preheated 350°F oven 7 to 9 minutes or until golden brown, stirring frequently.*

1. Lightly grease two 9-inch round cake pans. Line bottoms of pans with waxed paper. Prepare cake mix according to package directions, substituting coffee for water called for in directions. Pour batter into prepared pans; bake according to package directions. Cool cake layers in pans 15 minutes. Remove from pans; cool completely on wire racks.

2. Beat cream in medium bowl with electric mixer at high speed 1½ to 2 minutes or until soft peaks form. Add sugar, cocoa and vanilla; beat 15 to 20 seconds or until stiff peaks form. Cover with plastic wrap; refrigerate until ready to use.

3. Place one cake layer on serving plate. Stir raspberry jam until smooth; spread half of jam over cake layer. Top with second cake layer; spread with remaining jam. Frost top and side of cake with chocolate whipped cream.

4. Sprinkle half of almonds over top of cake; press remaining almonds into side of cake. Wrap loosely with plastic wrap; refrigerate until ready to serve. Garnish with fresh raspberries just before serving.          *Makes 12 servings*

# hidden surprise cake

1 package (about 16 ounces) angel food cake mix, plus ingredients
   to prepare mix
1½ to 2 pints chocolate ice cream, softened
2 cups cold whipping cream
¼ cup unsweetened cocoa powder
6 tablespoons powdered sugar
2 to 4 tablespoons mini chocolate chips (optional)

1. Prepare, bake and cool angel food cake mix according to package directions.

2. Place cake on work surface. Using serrated knife, cut horizontally across cake 1 inch from top. Remove top of cake; set aside.

3. Scoop out inside of cake, leaving 1-inch shell on side and bottom. (Be careful not to tear through cake.) Spoon ice cream into cake, packing down. Replace cake top.

4. Beat cream and cocoa in large bowl with electric mixer at medium speed until slightly thickened. Gradually beat in powdered sugar at high speed until stiff peaks form. Frost top and side of cake with chocolate whipped cream. Sprinkle with chocolate chips, if desired. Serve immediately.

*Makes 12 servings*

Note: The cake can be prepared and filled, without frosting, up to 1 week in advance. Wrap in heavy-duty foil and store in the freezer. Remove 15 minutes before frosting. Serve immediately after frosting.

# peppermint mountain range

1 package (about 18 ounces) white or yellow cake mix *without* pudding in the mix

1 package (4-serving size) vanilla instant pudding and pie filling mix

1 cup sour cream

4 eggs

$\frac{1}{2}$ cup vegetable oil

$\frac{1}{3}$ cup water

$\frac{3}{4}$ teaspoon peppermint extract

Red food coloring

1 cup mini chocolate chips

2 cups sifted powdered sugar

2 to 3 tablespoons milk

$\frac{1}{2}$ cup crushed peppermint candies (about 12 round candies)

1. Preheat oven to 350°F. Grease and flour 10- or 12-cup bundt pan.

2. Beat cake mix, pudding mix, sour cream, eggs, oil and water in large bowl with electric mixer at low speed 1 minute or until blended. Beat at medium speed 1 to 2 minutes or until smooth.

3. Combine 1$\frac{1}{2}$ cups batter, peppermint extract and 16 drops red food coloring in small bowl; mix well. Stir chocolate chips into remaining batter. Spread half of chocolate chip batter in prepared pan; top with peppermint batter. Spread remaining chocolate chip batter over peppermint batter.

4. Bake 50 to 60 minutes or until toothpick inserted near center comes out clean. Cool cake in pan 20 minutes. Invert onto wire rack; cool completely.

5. Blend powdered sugar and 2 tablespoons milk in small bowl until smooth. Add remaining milk, if necessary, to reach drizzling consistency. Drizzle glaze over cake; sprinkle with crushed candies. *Makes 12 servings*

# tres leches cake

1 package (about 18 ounces) white cake mix, plus ingredients
   to prepare mix
1 can (14 ounces) sweetened condensed milk
1 cup milk
1 cup whipping cream
1 container (8 ounces) whipped topping, thawed
   Fresh fruit (optional)

1. Preheat oven to 350°F. Spray 13×9-inch baking pan with nonstick
cooking spray.

2. Prepare cake mix according to package directions. Bake 35 to
40 minutes or until toothpick inserted into center comes out clean.
Cool cake in pan 5 minutes.

3. Meanwhile, combine sweetened condensed milk, milk and cream in
medium bowl. Poke holes all over warm cake with wooden skewer or
toothpick. Slowly pour milk mixture evenly over top of cake. Let cake
stand 10 to 15 minutes to absorb liquid. Cover and refrigerate cake at
least 1 hour.

4. When completely cool, spread whipped topping evenly over cake.
Garnish with fresh fruit. Store cake covered in refrigerator.

*Makes 12 to 15 servings*

# chocolate-covered coconut almond cake

¾ cup sliced almonds, toasted,* divided
1 package (about 18 ounces) yellow cake mix
1 package (4-serving size) vanilla instant pudding and pie filling mix
4 eggs
1 cup sour cream
¾ cup water
¼ cup vegetable oil
½ teaspoon vanilla
½ teaspoon coconut extract
⅔ cup shredded coconut, divided
½ cup whipping cream
½ cup semisweet or bittersweet chocolate chips

*To toast almonds, spread in single layer on baking sheet. Bake in preheated 350°F oven 7 to 9 minutes or until golden brown, stirring frequently.

1. Preheat oven to 350°F. Spray 10- or 12-cup bundt pan with nonstick cooking spray. Coarsely chop ½ cup almonds.

2. Beat cake mix, pudding mix, eggs, sour cream, water, oil, vanilla and coconut extract in large bowl with electric mixer at low speed 30 seconds. Beat at medium speed 2 minutes or until smooth. Fold in chopped almonds and ⅓ cup coconut. Pour batter into prepared pan.

3. Bake 1 hour or until toothpick inserted near center comes out clean. Cool cake in pan 10 minutes. Invert onto wire rack; cool completely.

4. Heat cream in small saucepan just until hot (do not boil). Remove saucepan from heat, add chocolate chips and let stand 2 minutes. Whisk until smooth. Let stand at room temperature 15 to 20 minutes or until slightly thickened. Stir; pour glaze over cake. Sprinkle with remaining ¼ cup almonds and ⅓ cup coconut. Refrigerate until ready to serve.

*Makes 12 servings*

# key lime angel food torte

1 package (about 16 ounces) angel food cake mix, plus ingredients
    to prepare mix
1 can (14 ounces) sweetened condensed milk
⅔ cup bottled key lime juice
1 container (8 ounces) whipped topping, thawed
⅓ cup shredded coconut
    Peel of 1 lime

1. Preheat oven to 350°F. Prepare and bake cake mix according to package directions in ungreased tube pan. Invert pan on wire rack; cool cake completely in pan.

2. For key lime filling, whisk sweetened condensed milk and lime juice in medium bowl until smooth. Fold in whipped topping. Cover and refrigerate until ready to use.

3. Loosen side of cake with knife; remove cake from pan. With bottom side up, cut cake in half horizontally with serrated knife. Cut each half in half to create four layers.

4. To assemble torte, place bottom cake layer cut side up on serving platter; spread with one fourth of key lime filling (about 1 cup). Repeat layers two times. Place top cake layer over filling; spread with remaining filling, allowing some to run down side of cake. Sprinkle with coconut and lime peel; refrigerate 1 hour or until set. *Makes 12 servings*

Tip: When making an angel food cake, it's important to not grease the pan so that the batter can grip the side of the pan and rise as high as possible. Using a tube pan with a removable bottom will make releasing the cake much easier.

# peanut butter & cookie cake

1 package (about 18 ounces) white cake mix
1 package (4-serving size) vanilla instant pudding and pie filling mix
4 eggs
½ cup milk
⅓ cup vegetable oil
¼ cup water
¼ cup creamy peanut butter
2 cups chopped peanut butter cookies, divided
½ cup semisweet chocolate chips
1 teaspoon shortening

1. Preheat oven to 350°F. Spray 12-cup bundt pan with nonstick cooking spray.

2. Beat cake mix, pudding mix, eggs, milk, oil, water and peanut butter in large bowl with electric mixer at medium speed 2 minutes or until well blended. Stir in 1¾ cups chopped cookies. Pour batter into prepared pan.

3. Bake 50 to 60 minutes or until cake springs back when lightly touched. Cool cake in pan 10 minutes. Invert onto wire rack; cool completely.

4. Combine chocolate chips and shortening in small microwavable bowl. Microwave on HIGH 1 minute; stir. Microwave at additional 15-second intervals until melted and smooth. Spoon glaze over cake; sprinkle with remaining ¼ cup chopped cookies.      *Makes 10 to 12 servings*

# mini neapolitan ice cream cakes

  1 package (about 18 ounces) vanilla cake mix
  ¾ cup water
  3 eggs
  ⅓ cup vegetable oil
  ⅓ cup unsweetened cocoa powder
  4 cups slightly softened strawberry ice cream
    Powdered sugar, dark chocolate curls and strawberries (optional)

1. Preheat oven to 350°F. Spray four mini (5×3-inch) loaf pans with nonstick cooking spray.

2. Beat cake mix, water, eggs and oil in large bowl with electric mixer at low speed 30 seconds. Beat at medium speed 2 minutes or until well blended. Reserve 1¾ cups batter. Add cocoa to remaining batter; stir until well blended.

3. Divide chocolate batter evenly between two prepared pans. Divide reserved plain batter evenly between remaining two prepared pans.

4. Bake 30 minutes or until toothpick inserted into centers comes out clean. Cool cakes in pans 10 minutes. Remove from pans; cool completely on wire racks.

5. Trim rounded tops of cakes with serrated knife. Cut each cake in half horizontally. Line 4 clean mini loaf pans with plastic wrap, leaving 2-inch overhang on all sides. Place 1 vanilla cake layer in each pan.

6. Place ice cream in large bowl; beat with electric mixer at medium speed 30 seconds or just until spreadable. Spread 1 cup ice cream over each vanilla cake layer in pans; top with chocolate cake layers. Cover tops of cakes with plastic wrap. Freeze at least 4 hours.

7. Remove cakes from loaf pans; trim any uneven sides. To serve, cut each cake into 3 slices. Garnish with powdered sugar, chocolate curls and strawberries.                    *Makes 4 cakes (12 servings)*

# carrot snack cake

1 package (about 18 ounces) butter recipe yellow cake mix with
pudding in the mix, plus ingredients to prepare mix

1½ cups chopped walnuts, divided

1 cup shredded carrots

2 jars (4 ounces each) strained carrot baby food

½ cup golden raisins

1½ teaspoons ground cinnamon

1½ teaspoons vanilla, divided

1 package (8 ounces) cream cheese, softened

Grated peel of 1 lemon

2 teaspoons lemon juice

3 cups powdered sugar

1. Preheat oven to 350°F. Grease 13×9-inch baking pan.

2. Prepare cake mix according to package directions but use only ½ cup
water instead of amount called for in directions. Stir 1 cup walnuts, carrots,
carrot baby food, raisins, cinnamon and ½ teaspoon vanilla into batter.
Spread batter in prepared pan.

3. Bake 40 minutes or until cake begins to pull away from sides of pan and
toothpick inserted into center comes out clean. Cool completely in pan on
wire rack.

4. Beat cream cheese in large bowl with electric mixer at medium speed
until fluffy. Beat in lemon peel, lemon juice and remaining 1 teaspoon
vanilla. Gradually add powdered sugar; beat until well blended. Spread
frosting over cake; sprinkle with remaining ½ cup walnuts. Refrigerate
2 hours before serving. *Makes 24 servings*

# chai spice cake

2¼ cups water
10 chai tea bags
1 cup ice cubes
1 package (about 18 ounces) white cake mix
3 egg whites
⅓ cup vegetable oil
1 tablespoon cornstarch
¼ cup packed brown sugar
6 whole cloves
½ teaspoon vanilla

**1.** Preheat oven to 350°F. Spray bottom only of 10- or 12-cup nonstick bundt or tube pan with nonstick cooking spray.

**2.** Bring water to a boil in medium saucepan over high heat. Remove from heat; add tea bags and steep 5 minutes. Remove and discard tea bags. Add ice cubes to saucepan; let stand until ice is completely melted. (This should make 2¼ cups tea.)

**3.** Beat cake mix, 1¼ cups tea, egg whites and oil in large bowl with electric mixer at low speed 30 seconds. Beat at medium speed 2 minutes or until well blended. Pour batter into prepared pan. Bake according to package directions or until toothpick inserted near center comes out clean. Cool cake in pan 10 minutes. Invert onto wire rack; cool completely.

**4.** Meanwhile, combine remaining 1 cup tea and cornstarch in medium saucepan; stir until cornstarch is completely dissolved. Add brown sugar and cloves; bring to a boil over medium-high heat, stirring constantly. Boil 1 minute, stirring constantly. Remove from heat; cool completely. Discard cloves; stir in vanilla. Pour glaze evenly over cake. *Makes 12 servings*

# classic chocolate-buttermilk birthday cake

1 package (about 18 ounces) chocolate fudge cake mix
1 package (4-serving size) chocolate instant pudding and pie filling mix
1⅓ cups buttermilk
4 eggs
½ cup vegetable oil
2 tablespoons unsweetened cocoa powder
2 teaspoons vanilla, divided
1½ cups sugar
1 cup whipping cream
½ cup (1 stick) butter, cubed
6 ounces unsweetened chocolate, chopped

1. Preheat oven to 350°F. Spray two 9-inch round cake pans with nonstick cooking spray.

2. Beat cake mix, pudding mix, buttermilk, eggs, oil, cocoa and 1 teaspoon vanilla in large bowl with electric mixer at low speed 1 minute. Beat at medium speed 2 minutes or until smooth and fluffy. Pour batter into prepared pans.

3. Bake 25 to 30 minutes or until toothpick inserted into centers comes out clean. Cool cake layers in pans 10 minutes. Remove from pans; cool completely on wire racks.

4. For frosting, stir sugar and cream in small saucepan over medium-high heat until sugar is dissolved. When cream begins to bubble, reduce heat and simmer 5 minutes. Remove from heat; stir in butter and chocolate until melted and smooth. Stir in remaining 1 teaspoon vanilla. Pour into medium bowl; refrigerate until frosting is cool and thickened.

5. Place 1 cake layer on plate; spread with frosting. Top with second cake layer; frost top and side of cake with remaining frosting. Refrigerate at least 1 hour before serving. Refrigerate leftovers.          *Makes 16 servings*

# easy lemon cake roll

½ cup powdered sugar
1 package (about 16 ounces) angel food cake mix
1¼ cups water
½ cup powdered sugar
2 cups cold milk
1 package (4-serving size) lemon instant pudding and pie filling mix
1 container (12 ounces) whipped topping, thawed
2 to 3 drops yellow food coloring (optional)
1½ cups shredded coconut

1. Preheat oven to 350°F. Spray 17×12-inch jelly-roll pan with nonstick cooking spray; line with waxed paper. **Sprinkle** clean towel with powdered sugar; set aside.

2. Beat cake mix and water in large bowl according to package directions. Pour batter into prepared pan. Bake 17 minutes or until toothpick inserted into center comes out clean. Immediately invert cake onto prepared towel. Fold towel edge over cake edge and roll up cake with towel jelly-roll style into 12-inch-long roll. Place seam side down on wire rack to cool completely (about 1 hour).

3. Stir milk into pudding mix in medium bowl. Whisk 2 minutes or until thickened. Gently fold in whipped topping and food coloring, if desired. Refrigerate until ready to use.

4. Slowly and carefully unroll cake onto serving plate, removing towel. Reserve 1 cup pudding mixture; spread remaining pudding mixture evenly over cake. Re-roll cake; place roll seam side down on platter. (If cake breaks, hold pieces together and continue to roll. Breaks can be hidden with frosting.) Frost cake with reserved 1 cup pudding mixture; sprinkle with coconut. Cut 1 inch off each end of cake with serrated knife; discard scraps. Cover with plastic wrap; refrigerate 2 to 3 hours before serving.

*Makes 10 servings*

# Crazy for
## Cupcakes

# carrot cream cheese cupcakes

1 package (8 ounces) cream cheese, softened
¼ cup powdered sugar
1 package (about 18 ounces) spice cake mix, plus ingredients
    to prepare mix
2 cups grated carrots
2 tablespoons finely chopped candied ginger
1 container (16 ounces) cream cheese frosting
3 tablespoons maple syrup
    Orange peel strips (optional)

1. Preheat oven to 350°F. Line 14 jumbo (3½-inch) muffin cups with paper or foil baking cups.

2. Beat cream cheese and powdered sugar in large bowl with electric mixer at medium speed 1 minute or until light and fluffy.

3. Prepare cake mix according to package directions; stir in carrots and ginger. Spoon batter into prepared muffin cups, filling one-third full (about ¼ cup batter). Place 1 tablespoon cream cheese mixture in center of each cup. Top with remaining batter (muffin cups should be two-thirds full).

4. Bake 25 to 28 minutes or until toothpick inserted into centers comes out clean. Cool cupcakes in pans 10 minutes. Remove from pans; cool completely on wire racks.

5. Mix frosting and maple syrup until well blended. Frost tops of cupcakes; garnish with orange peel. *Makes 14 jumbo cupcakes*

# chocolate cherry cupcakes

1 package (about 18 ounces) devil's food cake mix *without* pudding in the mix
1⅓ cups water
3 eggs
½ cup sour cream
⅓ cup vegetable oil
1 cup dried cherries
1 container (16 ounces) vanilla frosting, divided
   Green food coloring
11 maraschino cherries, stemmed and cut into halves

1. Preheat oven to 350°F. Line 22 standard (2½-inch) muffin cups with paper baking cups.

2. Beat cake mix, water, eggs, sour cream and oil in large bowl with electric mixer at low speed 30 seconds or until just blended. Beat at medium speed 2 minutes or until smooth. Fold in dried cherries. Spoon batter into prepared muffin cups, filling three-fourths full.

3. Bake 20 to 24 minutes or until toothpick inserted into centers comes out clean. Cool cupcakes in pans 10 minutes. Remove from pans; cool completely on wire racks.

4. Place ¼ cup frosting in small bowl; stir in food coloring, one drop at a time, until desired shade of green is reached.

5. Frost cupcakes with remaining frosting. Place 1 cherry half, cut side down, onto each cupcake. Place green frosting in piping bag fitted with writing tip. Pipe cherry stem and leaf onto each cupcake.

*Makes 22 cupcakes*

# surprise package cupcakes

1 package (about 18 ounces) cake mix, any flavor, plus ingredients
    to prepare mix
1 container (16 ounces) vanilla frosting
    Food coloring (optional)
1 tube white decorating icing
72 chewy fruit squares
    Colored decors

1. Preheat oven to 350°F. Spray 24 standard (2½-inch) muffin cups with nonstick cooking spray or line with paper baking cups.

2. Prepare and bake cake mix in prepared muffin cups according to package directions. Cool cupcakes in pans 15 minutes. Remove from pans; cool completely on wire racks.

3. Blend frosting and food coloring in medium bowl until desired shade is reached. Spread frosting over cupcakes.

4. Use icing to pipe "ribbons" on fruit squares to resemble wrapped presents. Arrange 3 candy presents on each cupcake. Decorate with decors. *Makes 24 cupcakes*

# triple-chocolate cupcakes

1 package (18¼ ounces) chocolate cake mix
1 package (4 ounces) chocolate instant pudding and pie filling mix
1 container (8 ounces) sour cream
4 large eggs
½ cup vegetable oil
½ cup warm water
2 cups (12-ounce package) NESTLÉ® TOLL HOUSE® Semi-Sweet
　　Chocolate Morsels
2 containers (16 ounces *each*) prepared frosting
　　Assorted candy sprinkles

**PREHEAT** oven to 350°F. Grease or paper-line 30 muffin cups.

**COMBINE** cake mix, pudding mix, sour cream, eggs, vegetable oil and water in large mixer bowl; beat on low speed just until blended. Beat on high speed for 2 minutes. Stir in morsels. Pour into prepared muffin cups, filling two-thirds full.

**BAKE** for 25 to 28 minutes or until wooden pick inserted in centers comes out clean. Cool in pans for 10 minutes; remove to wire racks to cool completely. Frost; decorate with candy sprinkles.　　*Makes 30 cupcakes*

If you bake cupcakes for the holidays, vary your baking cups and sprinkles to match the occasion. Use pink for Valentine's Day; red, white and blue for Independence Day; and orange and black for Halloween.

# white chocolate macadamia cupcakes

1½ cups shredded coconut
1 package (about 18 ounces) white cake mix *without* pudding in the mix, plus ingredients to prepare mix
1 package (4-serving size) white chocolate instant pudding and pie filling mix
¾ cup chopped macadamia nuts
1½ cups shredded coconut
1 cup white chocolate chips
1 container (16 ounces) white frosting

1. Preheat oven to 350°F. Line 20 standard (2½-inch) muffin cups with paper baking cups.

2. Spread coconut evenly on ungreased baking sheet; bake 6 minutes, stirring occasionally, until light golden brown. Cool completely; set aside.

3. Prepare cake mix according to package directions, adding pudding mix. Fold in macadamia nuts. Spoon batter into prepared muffin cups, filling two-thirds full.

4. Bake 18 to 20 minutes or until toothpick inserted into centers comes out clean. Cool cupcakes in pans 10 minutes. Remove from pans; cool completely on wire racks.

5. Place white chocolate chips in small microwavable bowl; microwave on MEDIUM (50%) 2 minutes, stirring every 30 seconds, until smooth. Cool slightly; stir into frosting. Frost cupcakes; sprinkle with toasted coconut.
*Makes 20 cupcakes*

# marshmallow fudge sundae cupcakes

1 package (about 18 ounces) chocolate cake mix, plus ingredients
to prepare mix
2 packages (4 ounces each) waffle bowls
40 large marshmallows
1 jar (8 ounces) hot fudge topping
1¼ cups whipped topping
¼ cup colored sprinkles
1 jar (10 ounces) maraschino cherries

1. Preheat oven to 350°F. Lightly spray 20 standard (2½-inch) muffin cups with nonstick cooking spray.

2. Prepare cake mix according to package directions. Spoon batter into prepared muffin cups, filling two-thirds full.

3. Bake 20 minutes or until toothpick inserted into centers comes out clean. Cool cupcakes in pans on wire racks 10 minutes.

4. Remove cupcakes from pans and place one cupcake in each waffle bowl. Place waffle bowls on ungreased baking sheets. Top each cupcake with 2 marshmallows; return to oven 2 minutes or until marshmallows are slightly softened.

5. Remove lid from fudge topping; microwave on HIGH 10 seconds or until softened. Top each cupcake with 2 teaspoons fudge topping, 1 tablespoon whipped topping, sprinkles and a cherry.          *Makes 20 cupcakes*

# boston cream cupcakes

1 package (about 18 ounces) yellow cake mix, plus ingredients
   to prepare mix
¼ cup French vanilla instant pudding and pie filling mix
1 cup cold milk
1 container (16 ounces) dark chocolate frosting

1. Preheat oven to 350°F. Lightly spray 22 standard (2½-inch) muffin cups with nonstick cooking spray.

2. Prepare and bake cake mix according to package directions for cupcakes. Cool cupcakes in pans 10 minutes. Remove from pans; cool completely on wire racks.

3. Meanwhile, whisk pudding mix and milk until well blended. Cover and refrigerate.

4. Gently poke small hole into bottom of each cupcake using tip of knife. Place pudding in pastry bag fitted with small round pastry tip.*

5. Place tip inside hole at bottom of cupcake; gently squeeze bag to fill cupcake with pudding. Repeat with remaining cupcakes and pudding.

6. Place frosting in medium microwavable bowl. Microwave on HIGH 30 seconds; stir. Frost tops of cupcakes.          *Makes 22 cupcakes*

*Or, use a plastic squeeze bottle with narrow dispensing tip.*

# black & whites

1 package (about 18 ounces) vanilla cake mix, plus ingredients
    to prepare mix
$\frac{2}{3}$ cup semisweet chocolate chips, melted and cooled slightly
4 ounces cream cheese, softened
1 cup prepared vanilla frosting
1 cup prepared chocolate frosting

1. Preheat oven to 350°F. Line 24 standard (2½-inch) muffin cups with paper baking cups.

2. Prepare cake mix according to package directions. Reserve half of batter (about 2½ cups) in medium bowl. Add melted chocolate and cream cheese to remaining batter; beat with electric mixer at medium speed 2 minutes or until smooth and well blended.

3. Spoon chocolate and vanilla batters side by side into prepared muffin cups, filling about two-thirds full. (Use chocolate batter first as it is slightly thicker and easier to position on one side of each muffin cup.)

4. Bake 16 minutes or until toothpick inserted into centers comes out clean. Cool cupcakes in pans 10 minutes. Remove from pans; cool completely on wire racks.

5. Spread vanilla frosting over half of each cupcake; spread chocolate frosting over remaining half of each cupcake.    *Makes 24 cupcakes*

# caramel apple cupcakes

1 package (about 18 ounces) butter recipe yellow cake mix,
    plus ingredients to prepare mix
1 cup chopped dried apples
    Caramel Frosting (recipe follows)
    Chopped nuts (optional)

1. Preheat oven to 375°F. Line 24 standard (2½-inch) muffin cups with paper baking cups.

2. Prepare cake mix according to package directions; stir in apples. Spoon batter into prepared muffin cups, filling two-thirds full.

3. Bake 15 to 20 minutes or until toothpick inserted into centers comes out clean. Cool cupcakes in pans 10 minutes. Remove from pans; cool completely on wire racks.

4. Prepare Caramel Frosting. Frost cupcakes; sprinkle with nuts, if desired.

*Makes 24 cupcakes*

Caramel Frosting: Melt 3 tablespoons butter in small saucepan. Stir in 1 cup packed light brown sugar, ½ cup evaporated milk and ⅛ teaspoon salt. Bring to a boil, stirring constantly. Remove from heat; cool slightly. Add 3¾ cups powdered sugar; beat until frosting is spreading consistency. Add ¾ teaspoon vanilla; beat until smooth.

# iced coffee cupcakes

1 package (about 18 ounces) chocolate fudge cake mix *without* pudding in the mix

1 package (4-serving size) chocolate instant pudding and pie filling mix

1⅓ cups brewed coffee, cooled to room temperature

3 eggs

½ cup vegetable oil

1 teaspoon vanilla

½ gallon mocha almond fudge or coffee ice cream, softened

1 bottle (7¼ ounces) quick-hardening chocolate shell dessert topping

½ cup pecan pieces, toasted

1. Preheat oven to 350°F. Line 20 standard (2½-inch) muffin cups with foil baking cups or spray with nonstick cooking spray.

2. Beat cake mix, pudding mix, coffee, eggs, oil and vanilla in large bowl with electric mixer at low speed 30 seconds. Beat at medium speed 2 minutes or until well blended and fluffy. Spoon into prepared muffin cups, filling three-fourths full.

3. Bake 15 to 20 minutes or until toothpick inserted into centers comes out clean. Cool cupcakes in pans 10 minutes. Remove from pans; cool completely on wire racks.

4. Working one at a time, remove 1 tablespoon cake from center of each cupcake top. Fill depression with 2 to 3 tablespoons ice cream, mounding on top. Spoon about 1 tablespoon dessert topping over ice cream; quickly sprinkle with pecans before topping hardens. Place cupcakes in freezer until ready to serve.

*Makes 20 cupcakes*

# ice cream cone cupcakes

1 package (about 18 ounces) white cake mix, plus ingredients
    to prepare mix
2 tablespoons nonpareils
24 flat-bottomed ice cream cones
    Prepared vanilla and chocolate frostings
    Additional nonpareils and decors

1. Preheat oven to 350°F.

2. Prepare cake mix according to package directions; stir in nonpareils. Stand cones in 13×9-inch baking pan or muffin cups. Spoon ¼ cup batter into each ice cream cone.

3. Bake 20 minutes or until toothpicks inserted into centers come out clean. Cool completely on wire racks.

4. Frost cupcakes and decorate as desired.     *Makes 24 cupcakes*

These cupcakes are best served the day they are prepared. If it is necessary to store them, cover them loosely.

# lemon-up cakes

1 package (about 18 ounces) butter recipe white cake mix with pudding in the mix, plus ingredients to prepare mix

1/2 cup lemon juice, divided (2 large lemons)

Grated peel of 2 lemons, divided

1/2 cup (1 stick) butter, softened

3 1/2 cups powdered sugar

Yellow food coloring

1 package (9 1/2 ounces) lemon-shaped hard candies, coarsely crushed

1. Preheat oven to 350°F. Spray 24 standard (2 1/2-inch) muffin cups with nonstick cooking spray or line with paper baking cups.

2. Prepare cake mix according to package directions but use 1/4 cup less water than called for in directions. Stir in 1/4 cup lemon juice and half of grated lemon peel. Spoon batter evenly into prepared muffin cups.

3. Bake 23 minutes or until light golden brown and toothpick inserted into centers comes out clean. Cool cupcakes in pans 5 minutes. Remove from pans; cool completely on wire racks.

4. Beat butter in large bowl with electric mixer at medium speed until creamy. Gradually add powdered sugar. Add remaining 1/4 cup lemon juice, lemon peel and several drops food coloring; beat at high speed until frosting is light and fluffy.

5. Frost cupcakes; sprinkle with crushed candies.          *Makes 24 cupcakes*

# cappuccino cupcakes

1 package (about 18 ounces) dark chocolate cake mix
1⅓ cups strong brewed or instant coffee, at room temperature
3 eggs
⅓ cup vegetable oil or melted butter
1 container (16 ounces) vanilla frosting
2 tablespoons coffee liqueur
Additional coffee liqueur (optional)
Grated chocolate*
Chocolate-covered coffee beans (optional)

*Grate half of a 3- or 4-ounce milk, dark or espresso chocolate candy bar on the large holes of a grater.

1. Preheat oven to 350°F. Line 24 standard (2½-inch) muffin cups with foil or paper baking cups.

2. Beat cake mix, coffee, eggs and oil in large bowl with electric mixer at low speed 30 seconds. Beat at medium speed 2 minutes. Spoon batter into prepared muffin cups, filling two-thirds full.

3. Bake 18 to 20 minutes or until toothpick inserted into centers comes out clean. Cool cupcakes in pans 10 minutes. Remove from pans; cool completely on wire racks. (At this point, cupcakes may be frozen for up to 3 months. Thaw at room temperature before frosting.)

4. Combine frosting and 2 tablespoons liqueur in small bowl; mix well. Before frosting, poke about 10 holes in each cupcake with toothpick. Pour 1 to 2 teaspoons liqueur over top of each cupcake, if desired. Frost and sprinkle with grated chocolate. Garnish with chocolate-covered coffee beans.

*Makes 24 cupcakes*

# banana split cupcakes

1 package (about 18 ounces) yellow cake mix, divided
1 cup water
1 cup mashed ripe bananas
3 eggs
1 cup chopped drained maraschino cherries
1½ cups mini chocolate chips, divided
1½ cups prepared vanilla frosting
1 cup marshmallow creme
1 teaspoon shortening
30 whole maraschino cherries, drained and patted dry

1. Preheat oven to 350°F. Line 30 standard (2½-inch) muffin cups with paper baking cups.

2. Reserve 2 tablespoons cake mix. Beat remaining cake mix, water, bananas and eggs in large bowl with electric mixer at low speed 30 seconds. Beat at medium speed 2 minutes. Combine chopped cherries and reserved cake mix in small bowl. Stir chopped cherry mixture and 1 cup chocolate chips into batter. Spoon batter into prepared muffin cups, filling two-thirds full.

3. Bake 15 to 20 minutes or until toothpick inserted into centers comes out clean. Cool cupcakes in pans 10 minutes. Remove from pans; cool completely on wire racks.

4. Combine frosting and marshmallow creme in medium bowl until well blended. Frost cupcakes.

5. Combine remaining ½ cup chocolate chips and shortening in small microwavable bowl. Microwave on HIGH 30 to 45 seconds, stirring after 30 seconds, or until smooth. Drizzle chocolate mixture over cupcakes. Place 1 whole cherry on each cupcake.                *Makes 30 cupcakes*

Variation: If desired, omit chocolate drizzle and top cupcakes with colored sprinkles.

# mini doughnut cupcakes

1 cup sugar
1½ teaspoons ground cinnamon
1 package (about 18 ounces) yellow or white cake mix,
  plus ingredients to prepare mix
1 tablespoon ground nutmeg

1. Preheat oven to 350°F. Grease and flour 48 mini (1¾-inch) muffin cups. Combine sugar and cinnamon in small bowl; set aside.

2. Prepare cake mix according to package directions; stir in nutmeg. Spoon batter into prepared muffin cups, filling two-thirds full.

3. Bake 12 minutes or until lightly browned and toothpick inserted into centers comes out clean.

4. Remove cupcakes from pans. Roll warm cupcakes in sugar mixture until completely coated.                    *Makes 48 mini cupcakes*

Use a nonstick cooking spray with flour added to make preparing the pans much quicker and easier.

# peanut butter & milk chocolate cupcakes

1 package (about 18 ounces) butter recipe yellow cake mix with pudding in the mix, plus ingredients to prepare mix
½ cup creamy peanut butter
¼ cup (½ stick) butter, softened
2 bars (3½ ounces each) good-quality milk chocolate, broken into small pieces
¼ cup (½ stick) unsalted butter, cut into small chunks
¼ cup whipping cream
Dash salt
Peanut butter chips

1. Preheat oven to 350°F. Line 24 standard (2½-inch) muffin cups with paper baking cups.

2. Prepare cake mix according to package directions, using ½ cup peanut butter and ¼ cup softened butter instead of ½ cup butter called for in directions. Fill muffin cups evenly with batter.

3. Bake 24 to 26 minutes or until light golden brown and toothpick inserted into centers comes out clean. Cool cupcakes in pans 5 minutes. Remove from pans; cool completely on wire racks.

4. Combine chocolate, unsalted butter, cream and salt in small, heavy saucepan. Heat over very low heat, stirring constantly, just until butter and chocolate melt. Mixture should be warm, not hot. Immediately spoon about 1 tablespoon chocolate glaze over each cupcake, spreading to cover top. Sprinkle with peanut butter chips. *Makes 24 cupcakes*

# lemon poppy seed cupcakes

1½ packages (12 ounces) cream cheese, softened
1½ cups plus ⅓ cup powdered sugar, divided
1 package (about 18 ounces) lemon cake mix, plus ingredients
    to prepare mix
1 tablespoon poppy seeds
    Grated peel and juice of 1 lemon
    Candied violets (optional)

1. Preheat oven to 350°F. Line 18 standard (2½-inch) muffin cups with paper baking cups.

2. Beat cream cheese and ⅓ cup powdered sugar in medium bowl with electric mixer at medium speed 1 minute or until light and fluffy.

3. Prepare cake mix according to package directions; stir in poppy seeds. Spoon 2 tablespoons batter into each prepared muffin cup. Place 2 teaspoons cream cheese mixture in center; top with 2 tablespoons batter.

4. Bake 22 to 24 minutes or until cupcakes spring back when lightly touched. Cool cupcakes in pans 10 minutes. Remove from pans; cool completely on wire racks.

5. Combine remaining 1½ cups powdered sugar, lemon peel and lemon juice in small bowl until well blended. Drizzle glaze over cupcakes or dip tops of cupcakes into glaze to cover completely. Garnish each cupcake with candied violet. *Makes 18 cupcakes*

# mini tiramisu cupcakes

1 package (about 18 ounces) yellow cake mix, plus ingredients
    to prepare mix
4 teaspoons instant espresso powder, divided
1 cup warm water
8 ounces mascarpone cheese,* softened
1 cup whipping cream
3 tablespoons powdered sugar
    Chocolate shavings or cocoa powder (optional)

*Mascarpone cheese is an Italian soft cheese (similar to cream cheese) that is a traditional ingredient in tiramisu. Look for it in the specialty cheese section of the supermarket.

1. Preheat oven to 350°F. Grease 48 mini (1¾-inch) muffin cups or line with paper baking cups.

2. Prepare cake mix according to package directions, reducing oil to 2 tablespoons. Spoon batter into prepared muffin cups, filling two-thirds full.

3. Bake 15 minutes or until toothpick inserted into centers comes out clean. Remove cupcakes from pans to wire racks. Use toothpicks to poke several holes in tops of cupcakes. Leave out overnight, uncovered, to dry out.

4. At least 1 hour before serving, dissolve 3 teaspoons espresso powder in water. Dip tops of cupcakes in espresso.

5. Beat mascarpone in medium bowl with electric mixer at medium speed until fluffy. If mascarpone separates, continue beating until it comes back together.

6. Beat cream, powdered sugar and remaining 1 teaspoon espresso powder in another medium bowl with electric mixer at medium speed until stiff peaks form. Fold one fourth of whipped cream mixture into mascarpone; fold mascarpone mixture into remaining whipped cream mixture until blended. Frost cupcakes; garnish with chocolate shavings. Refrigerate until ready to serve.                         *Makes 48 mini cupcakes*

# graduation party cupcakes

1 package (about 18 ounces) white cake mix
1¼ cups water
⅓ cup vegetable oil
3 egg whites
1 container (16 ounces) white frosting
    Food coloring
22 chocolate squares
    Gummy candy strips
22 mini candy-coated chocolate pieces

1. Preheat oven to 325°F. Line 22 standard (2½-inch) muffin cups with paper baking cups.

2. Beat cake mix, water, oil and egg whites in large bowl with electric mixer at low speed 30 seconds. Beat at medium speed 2 minutes. (Batter will be slightly lumpy.) Add food coloring to match school colors; stir until desired shade is reached. Spoon batter into prepared muffin cups, filling two-thirds full.

3. Bake 17 to 20 minutes or until toothpick inserted into centers comes out clean. Cool cupcakes in pans 10 minutes. Remove from pans; cool completely on wire racks.

4. Place frosting in medium bowl. Add food coloring to match school colors; stir until desired shade is reached. Spread frosting over cupcakes.

5. Arrange chocolate square on top of frosting. Place small dab of frosting in center of square to attach candy strips for tassel. Use additional frosting to attach chocolate piece for button. *Makes 22 cupcakes*

# rocky road cupcakes

1 package (about 18 ounces) chocolate fudge cake mix
1⅓ cups water
3 eggs
¾ cup mini chocolate chips, divided
½ cup vegetable oil
1 container (16 ounces) chocolate frosting
1 cup mini marshmallows
⅔ cup walnut pieces
Hot fudge ice cream topping, heated, or chocolate syrup

1. Preheat oven to 325°F. Line 22 standard (2½-inch) muffin cups with paper baking cups.

2. Beat cake mix, water, eggs, ¼ cup chocolate chips and oil in large bowl with electric mixer at low speed 30 seconds. Beat at medium speed 2 minutes or until well blended. Spoon batter into prepared muffin cups, filling two-thirds full.

3. Bake 20 minutes or until toothpick inserted into centers comes out clean. Cool cupcakes in pans 10 minutes. Remove from pans; cool completely on wire racks.

4. Spread thin layer of frosting over cupcakes. Top with marshmallows, walnuts and remaining ½ cup chocolate chips, pressing down lightly to adhere to frosting. Drizzle with hot fudge topping.

*Makes 22 cupcakes*

# butterfly cupcakes

1 package (about 18 ounces) cake mix, any flavor, plus ingredients
    to prepare mix
1 container (16 ounces) white frosting
  Blue and green food coloring
  Assorted candies and colored sugar
  Red licorice strings, cut into 4-inch pieces

1. Preheat oven to 350°F. Lightly spray 24 standard (2½-inch) muffin cups with nonstick cooking spray.

2. Prepare cake mix according to package directions. Spoon batter into prepared muffin cups, filling two-thirds full.

3. Bake 20 minutes or until toothpick inserted into centers comes out clean. Cool cupcakes in pans 10 minutes. Remove from pans; cool completely on wire racks.

4. Divide frosting between 2 small bowls. Add food coloring to each bowl, 1 drop at a time, until desired shades of blue and green are reached.

5. Cut cupcakes in half vertically. Place halves together, cut sides out, to resemble butterfly wings. Frost cupcakes; decorate with candies and colored sugar as desired. Snip each end of licorice string pieces to form antennae; place in center of each cupcake. *Makes 24 cupcakes*

# lemon meringue cupcakes

1 package (about 18 ounces) lemon cake mix, plus ingredients
to prepare mix
¾ cup prepared lemon curd*
4 egg whites, at room temperature
6 tablespoons sugar

*Lemon curd, a thick sweet lemon spread, is available in many supermarkets where the jams and preserves are located.*

1. Preheat oven to 350°F. Line 9 jumbo (3½-inch) muffin cups with paper baking cups.

2. Prepare cake mix according to package directions. Spoon batter into prepared muffin cups, filling two-thirds full. Bake 23 to 25 minutes or until toothpick inserted into centers comes out clean. Cool cupcakes in pans 10 minutes. Remove from pans; cool on wire racks. *Increase oven temperature to 375°F.*

3. Use serrated knife to cut off tops of cupcakes even with tops of baking cups. (Do not remove paper baking cups.) Scoop out small hole in center of each cupcake using tablespoon; fill hole with generous tablespoon lemon curd. Replace cupcake tops.

4. Beat egg whites in medium bowl with electric mixer at high speed until soft peaks form. Continue beating while gradually adding sugar; beat until stiff peaks form. Pipe or spread meringue in peaks on each cupcake.

5. Place cupcakes on baking sheet. Bake 5 to 6 minutes or until peaks of meringue are golden.                    *Makes 9 jumbo cupcakes*

Variation: This recipe also makes 24 standard (2½-inch) cupcakes. Line muffin pans with paper baking cups; prepare and bake cake mix according to package directions. Cut off tops of cupcakes; scoop out hole in each cupcake with teaspoon and fill with generous teaspoon lemon curd. Pipe or spread meringue in peaks on each cupcake; bake as directed above.

# frosty chocolate-cherry treats

1 package (about 18 ounces) triple chocolate cake mix
1 package (4-serving size) chocolate instant pudding and pie
    filling mix
1 cup water
2 eggs
1 tablespoon instant coffee granules
1 teaspoon vanilla
2 pints cherry chip or chocolate-cherry chip ice cream, softened
5 egg whites
½ cup sugar
¼ teaspoon salt

1. Preheat oven 350°F. Spray eight 6-ounce custard cups with nonstick cooking spray. Place on rimmed baking sheet.

2. Beat cake mix, pudding mix, water, eggs, instant coffee and vanilla in large bowl with electric mixer at low speed 1 minute. Beat at medium speed 2 minutes or until well blended and fluffy (batter will be very thick). Pour ½ cup batter into each custard cup. Bake 20 to 25 minutes or until toothpick inserted into centers comes out clean. Cool cakes completely. Remove cakes from custard cups; place on rimmed baking sheet.

3. Place broiler rack 6 inches from heat; preheat broiler. Scoop about ⅓ cup ice cream on top of each cake; place in freezer while preparing meringue. Beat egg whites in medium bowl with electric mixer at high speed 1 to 2 minutes or until foamy. Gradually add sugar and salt; beat 5 minutes or until shiny and stiff. Working with 1 cake at a time, spread meringue over ice cream to edges of cake, mounding in center to create dome shape.

4. Broil 1 to 2 minutes or until meringue is lightly browned. Serve immediately.                    *Makes 8 servings*

# tropical luau cupcakes

2 cans (8 ounces each) crushed pineapple in juice

1 package (about 18 ounces) yellow cake mix *without* pudding in the mix

1 package (4-serving size) banana cream instant pudding and pie filling mix

4 eggs

⅓ cup vegetable oil

¼ teaspoon ground nutmeg

1 container (12 ounces) whipped vanilla frosting

¾ cup shredded coconut, toasted*

3 to 4 medium kiwi

30 (2½-inch) pretzel sticks

*To toast coconut, spread evenly on ungreased baking sheet. Toast in preheated 350°F oven 5 to 7 minutes, stirring occasionally, until light golden brown.*

1. Preheat oven to 350°F. Line 30 standard (2½-inch) muffin cups with paper baking cups. Drain pineapple, reserving juice. Set pineapple aside.

2. Beat cake mix, pudding mix, eggs, oil, reserved pineapple juice and nutmeg in large bowl with electric mixer at low speed 1 minute or until blended. Beat at medium speed 2 minutes or until smooth. Fold in pineapple. Spoon batter into prepared muffin cups, filling two-thirds full.

3. Bake 20 minutes or until toothpick inserted into centers comes out clean. Cool cupcakes in pans 5 minutes. Remove from pans; cool completely on wire racks.

4. Frost tops of cupcakes; sprinkle with coconut. For palm trees,* peel kiwi and cut into ⅛-inch-thick slices. Cut small notches around edges of slices to resemble palm fronds. For palm tree trunk, push pretzel stick into, but not through, center of each kiwi slice. Push other end of pretzel into top of each cupcake.                                                    *Makes 30 cupcakes*

*Palm tree decorations can be made up to 1 hour before serving.*

# pink lemonade cupcakes

1 package (about 18 ounces) white cake mix *without* pudding
    in the mix

1 cup water

3 egg whites

1/3 cup plus 1/4 cup thawed frozen pink lemonade concentrate, divided

2 tablespoons vegetable oil

5 to 8 drops red food coloring, divided

4 cups sifted powdered sugar

1/3 cup butter, softened

    Lemon slice candies (optional)

1. Preheat oven to 350°F. Line 24 standard (2½-inch) muffin cups with paper baking cups.

2. Beat cake mix, water, egg whites, 1/3 cup lemonade concentrate, oil and 4 to 6 drops food coloring in large bowl with electric mixer at medium speed 2 minutes. Spoon batter evenly into prepared muffin cups.

3. Bake 18 to 22 minutes or until toothpick inserted into centers comes out clean. Cool cupcakes in pans 5 minutes. Remove from pans; cool completely on wire racks.

4. Beat powdered sugar, butter and remaining 1/4 cup lemonade concentrate in medium bowl with electric mixer at medium speed until well blended. Beat in remaining food coloring until desired shade of pink is reached.

5. Spread frosting over cupcakes. Garnish with candies.

*Makes 24 cupcakes*

# Incredible

## Cookies

# moon rocks

  1 package (about 18 ounces) devil's food or German chocolate cake
      mix with pudding in the mix
  3 eggs
  ½ cup (1 stick) butter, melted
  2 cups slightly crushed (2½-inch) pretzel sticks
1½ cups uncooked old-fashioned oats
  1 cup swirled chocolate and white chocolate chips or candy-coated
      semisweet chocolate baking pieces

**1.** Preheat oven to 350°F.

**2.** Blend cake mix, eggs and butter in large bowl. Stir in pretzels, oats and chocolate chips. (Dough will be stiff.) Drop dough by rounded teaspoonfuls about 2 inches apart onto ungreased cookie sheets.

**3.** Bake 7 to 9 minutes or until set. Cool cookies on cookie sheets 1 minute; remove to wire racks to cool completely.          *Makes 5 dozen cookies*

# quick fruit & lemon drops

  ½ cup sugar
  1 package (about 18 ounces) lemon cake mix
  ⅓ cup water
  ¼ cup (½ stick) butter, softened
  1 egg
  1 tablespoon grated lemon peel
  1 cup mixed dried fruit bits

**1.** Preheat oven to 350°F. Grease cookie sheets. Place sugar in shallow bowl.

**2.** Beat cake mix, water, butter, egg and lemon peel in large bowl with electric mixer at low speed until well blended. Beat in fruit bits just until blended. Shape heaping tablespoonfuls of dough into balls; roll in sugar to coat. Place 2 inches apart on prepared cookie sheets.

3. Bake 12 to 14 minutes or until set. Cool cookies on cookie sheets 2 minutes; remove to wire racks to cool completely.

*Makes about 2 dozen cookies*

Tip: If dough is too sticky to handle, add about ¼ cup all-purpose flour.

# chocolate peanut butter cookies

½ cup (1 stick) butter, softened
½ cup plus ¼ cup creamy peanut butter, divided
1 egg
2 tablespoons water
1 package (about 18 ounces) chocolate cake mix with pudding in the mix
1 package (12 ounces) semisweet chocolate chips
¼ cup chopped peanuts

1. Preheat oven to 350°F. Line two cookie sheets with parchment paper.

2. Beat butter and ½ cup peanut butter in large bowl with electric mixer at medium speed until well blended. Add egg and water; beat until well blended. Beat in cake mix until well blended.

3. Shape level teaspoonfuls of dough into balls. Place on prepared cookie sheets; flatten to ⅓-inch thickness with bottom of glass dipped in sugar. Bake 12 to 15 minutes or until set. Cool cookies on cookie sheets 2 minutes; remove to wire racks to cool completely.

4. Melt chocolate chips and remaining ¼ cup peanut butter in top of double boiler, stirring occasionally. Stir in peanuts. Spread about 1 teaspoon mixture on each cookie. Let stand 2 hours or refrigerate 1 hour to allow frosting to set.

*Makes about 4 dozen cookies*

# coconut clouds

2⅔ cups flaked coconut, divided
1 package DUNCAN HINES® Moist Deluxe® Classic Yellow Cake Mix
1 egg
½ cup vegetable oil
¼ cup water
1 teaspoon almond extract

1. Preheat oven to 350°F. Reserve 1⅓ cups coconut in medium bowl.

2. Combine cake mix, egg, oil, water and almond extract in large bowl. Beat at low speed with electric mixer. Stir in remaining 1⅓ cups coconut. Drop rounded teaspoonful of dough into reserved coconut. Roll to cover lightly. Place on ungreased baking sheet. Repeat with remaining dough, placing balls 2 inches apart.

3. Bake at 350°F for 10 to 12 minutes or until light golden brown. Cool 1 minute on baking sheets. Remove to cooling racks. Cool completely. Store in airtight container.                    *Makes 3½ dozen cookies*

To save time when forming dough into balls, use a 1-inch spring-operated cookie scoop. Spring-operated cookie scoops are available at kitchen specialty shops.

# sweet mysteries

1 package (about 18 ounces) yellow cake mix with pudding in the mix
½ cup (1 stick) butter, softened
1 egg yolk
1 cup ground pecans
36 milk chocolate candy kisses, unwrapped
Powdered sugar

1. Preheat oven to 300°F.

2. Beat half of cake mix and butter in large bowl with electric mixer at high speed until blended. Add egg yolk and remaining cake mix; beat at medium speed just until dough forms. Stir in pecans.

3. Shape rounded tablespoonful of dough around each candy, making sure candy is completely covered. Place 1 inch apart on ungreased cookie sheets.

4. Bake 20 to 25 minutes or until set and just beginning to turn golden. Cool cookies on cookie sheets 10 minutes. Place waxed paper under wire racks. Remove cookies to wire racks; sprinkle with powdered sugar.

*Makes 3 dozen cookies*

# blondie biscotti with almonds

1 cup slivered almonds
1 package (about 18 ounces) white cake mix
$\frac{2}{3}$ cup all-purpose flour
2 eggs
3 tablespoons melted butter, cooled slightly
1 teaspoon vanilla
3 tablespoons grated lemon peel

1. Preheat oven to 350°F. Line cookie sheet with parchment paper.

2. Heat medium skillet over medium heat. Add almonds and cook $1\frac{1}{2}$ to 2 minutes or just until fragrant, stirring constantly. *Do not brown.* Set aside.

3. Beat cake mix, flour, eggs, butter and vanilla in large bowl with electric mixer at low speed 1 to 2 minutes or until well blended. Stir in almonds and lemon peel. Knead dough 7 to 8 times or until ingredients are well blended.

4. Divide dough in half. Shape each half into 12×2×$\frac{1}{2}$-inch log; place logs 3 inches apart on prepared cookie sheet.

5. Bake 25 minutes or until toothpick inserted into centers of logs comes out clean. Cool on cookie sheet on wire rack 25 minutes.

6. Remove biscotti logs to cutting board, peeling off parchment paper. Cut each log diagonally into $\frac{1}{2}$-inch slices with serrated knife. Place slices, cut sides down, on cookie sheet. Bake 10 minutes or until bottoms of slices are golden brown. Remove to wire racks to cool completely. Store in airtight container. *Makes about 3 dozen biscotti*

# garbage pail cookies

1 package (about 18 ounces) white cake mix with pudding in the mix
½ cup (1 stick) butter, softened
2 eggs
1 teaspoon ground cinnamon
1 teaspoon vanilla
½ cup peanut butter chips
½ cup salted peanuts
½ cup mini candy-coated chocolate pieces
1½ cups crushed salted potato chips

1. Preheat oven to 350°F. Lightly grease cookie sheets.

2. Beat half of cake mix, butter, eggs, cinnamon and vanilla in large bowl with electric mixer at medium speed until light. Beat in remaining cake mix until well blended. Stir in peanut butter chips, peanuts and candy-coated chocolate pieces. Stir in potato chips. (Dough will be stiff.) Drop batter by rounded tablespoonfuls 2 inches apart onto prepared cookie sheets.

3. Bake 15 minutes or until golden brown. Cool cookies on cookie sheets 2 minutes; remove to wire racks to cool completely.

*Makes about 3½ dozen cookies*

To soften butter quickly, place one stick of butter on a microwavable plate and heat on LOW (30%) about 30 seconds or just until softened.

# crispy thumbprint cookies

1 package (about 18 ounces) yellow cake mix
½ cup vegetable oil
¼ cup water
1 egg
3 cups crisp rice cereal, crushed
½ cup chopped walnuts
6 tablespoons raspberry or strawberry preserves

1. Preheat oven to 375°F.

2. Beat cake mix, oil, water and egg in large bowl with electric mixer at medium speed until well blended. Add cereal and walnuts; beat until well blended.

3. Drop dough by heaping teaspoonfuls about 2 inches apart onto ungreased cookie sheets. Use thumb to make indentation in each cookie. Spoon about ½ teaspoon preserves into center of each cookie.

4. Bake 9 to 11 minutes or until golden brown. Cool cookies on cookie sheets 1 minute; remove to wire racks to cool completely.

*Makes 3 dozen cookies*

Prep and Bake Time: **30 minutes**

# pinwheel cookies

½ cup shortening plus additional for greasing
⅓ cup plus 1 tablespoon butter, softened and divided
2 egg yolks
½ teaspoon vanilla extract
1 package DUNCAN HINES® Moist Deluxe® Fudge Marble Cake Mix

1. Combine ½ cup shortening, ⅓ cup butter, egg yolks and vanilla extract in large bowl. Mix at low speed with electric mixer until blended. Set aside cocoa packet from cake mix. Gradually add cake mix. Blend well.

2. Divide dough in half. Add cocoa packet and remaining 1 tablespoon butter to one half of dough. Knead until well blended and chocolate colored.

3. Roll out yellow dough between two pieces of waxed paper into 18×12×⅛-inch rectangle. Repeat with chocolate dough. Remove top pieces of waxed paper from chocolate and yellow doughs. Place yellow dough directly on top of chocolate dough. Remove remaining layers of waxed paper. Roll up jelly-roll fashion, beginning at wide side. Refrigerate 2 hours.

4. Preheat oven to 350°F. Grease baking sheets.

5. Cut dough into ⅛-inch slices. Place sliced dough 1 inch apart on prepared baking sheets. Bake at 350°F for 9 to 11 minutes or until lightly browned. Cool 5 minutes on baking sheets. Remove to cooling racks.

*Makes about 3½ dozen cookies*

# chocolate chip-oat cookies

1 package (about 18 ounces) yellow cake mix
1 teaspoon baking powder
¾ cup vegetable oil
2 eggs
1 teaspoon vanilla
1 cup uncooked old-fashioned oats
¾ cup semisweet chocolate chips

1. Preheat oven to 350°F. Lightly grease cookie sheets or line with parchment paper.

2. Combine cake mix and baking powder in large bowl. Add oil, eggs and vanilla; beat with electric mixer at low speed 3 minutes or until well blended. Stir in oats and chocolate chips.

3. Drop dough by slightly rounded tablespoonfuls 2 inches apart onto prepared cookie sheets.

4. Bake 10 minutes or until golden brown. Cool cookies on cookie sheets 5 minutes; remove to wire racks to cool completely.

*Makes 4 dozen cookies*

# quick chocolate softies

1 package (about 18 ounces) devil's food cake mix
⅓ cup water
¼ cup (½ stick) butter, softened
1 egg
1 cup white chocolate chips
½ cup coarsely chopped walnuts

1. Preheat oven to 350°F. Grease cookie sheets.

2. Beat cake mix, water, butter and egg in large bowl with electric mixer at low speed until moistened. Beat at medium speed 1 minute. (Dough will be stiff.) Stir in white chocolate chips and nuts; stir until well blended. Drop dough by heaping teaspoonfuls 2 inches apart onto prepared cookie sheets.

3. Bake 10 to 12 minutes or until set. Cool cookies on cookie sheets 1 minute; remove to wire racks to cool completely.

*Makes about 4 dozen cookies*

If you're baking several batches of cookies using the same cookie sheets, make sure to let the cookie sheets cool to room temperature before adding more dough. Hot cookie sheets will cause the dough to melt and spread, which can result in very flat and/or overbaked cookies.

# cinnamon cereal crispies

½ cup granulated sugar

2 teaspoons ground cinnamon, divided

1 package (about 18 ounces) white or yellow cake mix with pudding
   in the mix

½ cup water

⅓ cup vegetable oil

1 egg

2 cups crisp rice cereal

1 cup cornflakes

1 cup raisins

1 cup chopped nuts (optional)

1. Preheat oven to 350°F. Lightly spray cookie sheets with nonstick cooking spray. Combine sugar and 1 teaspoon cinnamon in small bowl.

2. Beat cake mix, water, oil, egg and remaining 1 teaspoon cinnamon in large bowl with electric mixer at medium speed 1 minute. Gently stir in rice cereal, cornflakes, raisins and nuts, if desired, until well blended. Drop dough by rounded tablespoonfuls 2 inches apart onto prepared cookie sheets. Sprinkle lightly with half of cinnamon-sugar mixture.

3. Bake 15 minutes or until lightly browned. Sprinkle cookies with remaining cinnamon-sugar mixture; remove to wire racks to cool completely.

*Makes about 5 dozen cookies*

# chocolate almond biscotti

1 package DUNCAN HINES® Moist Deluxe® Dark Chocolate Cake Mix
1 cup all-purpose flour
$\frac{1}{2}$ cup butter or margarine, melted
2 eggs
1 teaspoon almond extract
$\frac{1}{2}$ cup chopped almonds
White chocolate, melted (optional)

1. Preheat oven to 350°F. Line 2 baking sheets with parchment paper.

2. Combine cake mix, flour, butter, eggs and almond extract in large bowl. Beat at low speed with electric mixer until well blended; stir in almonds. Divide dough in half. Shape each half into 12×2-inch log; place logs on prepared baking sheets.

3. Bake at 350°F for 30 to 35 minutes or until toothpick inserted in center comes out clean. Remove logs from oven; cool on baking sheets 15 minutes. Using serrated knife, cut logs into $\frac{1}{2}$-inch slices. Arrange slices on baking sheets. Bake biscotti 10 minutes. Remove to cooling racks; cool completely.

4. Dip one end of each biscotti in melted white chocolate, if desired. Allow white chocolate to set at room temperature before storing biscotti in airtight container.                    *Makes about 2$\frac{1}{2}$ dozen cookies*

# sunshine sandwiches

⅓ cup coarse or granulated sugar
¾ cup (1½ sticks) plus 2 tablespoons butter, softened, divided
1 egg
2 tablespoons grated lemon peel
1 package (about 18 ounces) lemon cake mix with pudding in the mix
¼ cup yellow cornmeal
2 cups sifted powdered sugar
2 to 3 tablespoons lemon juice

1. Preheat oven to 375°F. Place coarse sugar in shallow bowl.

2. Beat ¾ cup butter in large bowl with electric mixer at medium speed until fluffy. Add egg and lemon peel; beat 30 seconds. Add cake mix, one third at a time, beating at low speed after each addition until combined. Stir in cornmeal. (Dough will be stiff.)

3. Shape dough into 1-inch balls; roll in sugar to coat. Place 2 inches apart on ungreased cookie sheets.

4. Bake 8 to 9 minutes or until bottoms begin to brown. Cool cookies on cookie sheets 1 minute; remove to wire racks to cool completely.

5. Meanwhile, beat powdered sugar and remaining 2 tablespoons butter in small bowl with electric mixer at low speed until blended. Gradually add enough lemon juice to reach spreading consistency.

6. Spread 1 slightly rounded teaspoonful frosting on bottom of one cookie. Top with second cookie, bottom side down. Repeat with remaining cookies and frosting. Store covered at room temperature for up to 24 hours or freeze.                    *Makes 1½ dozen sandwich cookies*

# cranberry gems

⅔ cup dried cranberries or dried cherries
½ cup granulated sugar
3 tablespoons water, divided
1 package (about 18 ounces) white cake mix with pudding in the mix
2 eggs
2 tablespoons vegetable oil
¼ teaspoon almond extract or vanilla
½ cup powdered sugar
1 to 2 teaspoons milk

1. Preheat oven to 350°F. Lightly grease cookie sheets.

2. Combine cranberries, granulated sugar and 1 tablespoon water in small microwavable bowl. Microwave on HIGH 1 minute; let cranberries stand 10 minutes before draining.

3. Blend cake mix, eggs, remaining 2 tablespoons water, oil and almond extract in large bowl until smooth. Drop dough by rounded teaspoonfuls 2 inches apart onto prepared cookie sheets. Top each cookie with several cranberries.

4. Bake 10 minutes or until edges are lightly browned. Top each cookie with 1 or 2 additional cranberries after baking. Remove to wire racks to cool completely.

5. Blend powdered sugar and 1 teaspoon milk in small bowl until smooth. Add additional milk if necessary to reach drizzling consistency. Drizzle glaze over cookies.                    *Makes about 5 dozen cookies*

# pastel mint swirls

⅓ cup coarse or granulated sugar
1 package (about 18 ounces) devil's food cake mix *without* pudding
    in the mix
3 eggs
¼ cup (½ stick) butter, melted
¼ cup unsweetened cocoa powder
144 pastel mint chips

1. Preheat oven to 375°F. Place sugar in shallow bowl.

2. Combine cake mix, eggs, butter and cocoa in large bowl just until blended. (Dough will be stiff.)

3. Shape dough into 1-inch balls; roll in sugar to coat. Place 2 inches apart on ungreased cookie sheets.

4. Bake 8 to 9 minutes or until tops are cracked. Gently press 3 mint chips into top of each cookie. Cool cookies on cookie sheets 1 minute; remove to wire racks to cool completely.　　　*Makes 4 dozen cookies*

# whoopie pies

1 package (about 18 ounces) devil's food cake mix *without*
    pudding in the mix
1 package (4-serving size) chocolate instant pudding and
    pie filling mix
1 cup water
4 eggs
1¼ cups (2½ sticks) butter, softened, divided
1¼ cups marshmallow creme
¾ cup powdered sugar
½ teaspoon vanilla

1. Preheat oven to 350°F. Grease cookie sheets.

2. For cookies, beat cake mix, pudding mix, water, eggs and ½ cup butter in large bowl with electric mixer at low speed until just moistened. Beat at medium speed 2 minutes or until light and thick, scraping down side of bowl frequently. Drop batter by heaping tablespoonfuls 2 inches apart onto prepared cookie sheets.

3. Bake 12 to 14 minutes or until cookies spring back when touched lightly. (Cookies should be about 3 inches in diameter after baking.) Cool cookies on cookie sheets 5 minutes; remove to wire racks to cool completely.

4. Meanwhile, for filling, beat remaining ¾ cup butter, marshmallow creme, powdered sugar and vanilla in large bowl with electric mixer at high speed 2 minutes or until light and fluffy.

5. Spread filling on flat side of half of cookies; top with remaining cookies.
*Makes about 2 dozen sandwich cookies*

# chocolate chip 'n oatmeal cookies

1 package (18.25 or 18.5 ounces) yellow cake mix
1 cup quick-cooking rolled oats, uncooked
¾ cup (1½ sticks) butter or margarine, softened
2 eggs
1 cup HERSHEY'S SPECIAL DARK™ Chocolate Chips or HERSHEY'S
    Semi-Sweet Chocolate Chips

1. Heat oven to 350°F.

2. Combine cake mix, oats, butter and eggs in large bowl; mix well. Stir in chocolate chips. Drop by rounded teaspoons onto ungreased cookie sheets.

3. Bake 10 to 12 minutes or until very lightly browned. Cool slightly; remove from cookie sheets to wire racks. Cool completely.

*Makes about 4 dozen cookies*

# black and white sandwich cookies

1 package (about 18 ounces) chocolate cake mix with pudding in the mix
1½ cups (3 sticks) butter, softened, divided
2 egg yolks
½ to ¾ cup milk, divided
1 package (about 18 ounces) butter recipe yellow cake mix with pudding in the mix
4 cups powdered sugar
¼ teaspoon salt

1. Preheat oven to 325°F. For chocolate cookies, beat half of chocolate cake mix and ½ cup butter in large bowl with electric mixer at high speed until well blended. Add 1 egg yolk and remaining chocolate cake mix; beat just until dough forms. Beat in 1 to 2 tablespoons milk if dough is too crumbly.

2. Shape dough by rounded tablespoonfuls into 36 balls. Place 2 inches apart on ungreased cookie sheets; flatten slightly. Bake 20 minutes or until cookies are set. Cool cookies on cookie sheets 5 minutes; remove to wire racks to cool completely.

3. For vanilla cookies, beat half of yellow cake mix and ½ cup butter in another large bowl with electric mixer at high speed until well blended. Add remaining egg yolk and yellow cake mix; beat just until dough forms. Beat in 1 to 2 tablespoons milk if dough is too crumbly.

4. Shape dough by rounded tablespoonfuls into 36 balls. Place 2 inches apart on ungreased cookie sheets; flatten slightly. Bake 20 minutes or until cookies are set. Cool cookies on cookie sheets 5 minutes; remove to wire racks to cool completely.

5. Cut remaining ½ cup butter into small pieces. Beat butter, powdered sugar, salt and 6 tablespoons milk in large bowl with electric mixer until light and fluffy. Add additional 2 tablespoons milk, if necessary, for more spreadable frosting. Spread frosting on flat sides of chocolate cookies. Top with vanilla cookies.                     *Makes 3 dozen sandwich cookies*

# hermits

6 tablespoons butter, softened
¼ cup packed dark brown sugar
1 egg
1 package (about 18 ounces) yellow cake mix with pudding in the mix
⅓ cup molasses
1 teaspoon ground cinnamon
¼ teaspoon baking soda
¾ cup raisins
¾ cup chopped pecans
2½ tablespoons maple syrup
1 tablespoon butter, melted
¼ teaspoon maple flavoring
¾ cup powdered sugar

1. Preheat oven to 375°F. Line two cookie sheets with parchment paper.

2. Beat softened butter and brown sugar in large bowl with electric mixer at medium-high speed until well blended. Beat in egg. Add cake mix, molasses, cinnamon and baking soda; beat just until blended. Stir in raisins and pecans. Drop dough by rounded tablespoonfuls 1½ inches apart onto prepared cookie sheets.

3. Bake 13 to 15 minutes or until set. Cool cookies on cookie sheets 5 minutes; remove to wire racks to cool completely.

4. For glaze, combine maple syrup, melted butter and maple flavoring in medium bowl. Add powdered sugar, ¼ cup at a time, stirring until smooth. Drizzle glaze over cookies. Let stand 30 minutes or until glaze is set.

*Makes about 4 dozen cookies*

# cappuccino cookies

1 package (about 18 ounces) devil's food cake mix
¾ cup milk
8 egg whites
1 tablespoon instant coffee granules
1 teaspoon ground cinnamon

**1.** Preheat oven to 400°F. Lightly spray cookie sheets with nonstick cooking spray.

**2.** Combine cake mix, milk, egg whites, instant coffee and cinnamon in medium bowl with spatula until well blended. Drop dough by rounded teaspoonfuls onto prepared cookie sheets.

**3.** Bake 5 minutes or until centers are set. Remove cookies to wire racks to cool completely.

*Makes 4 dozen cookies*

Eggs separate more easily when they are cold. Crack the eggs gently against a flat surface, such as a countertop, rather than the edge of a bowl—this allows a cleaner break, so you are less likely to end up with bits of eggshell falling into the bowl with the egg whites.

# Very Best

*Bars*

# jam jam bars

1 package (about 18 ounces) yellow or white cake mix with pudding in the mix
½ cup (1 stick) butter, melted
1 cup apricot preserves or raspberry jam
1 package (11 ounces) peanut butter and milk chocolate chips

1. Preheat oven to 350°F. Lightly spray 13×9-inch baking pan with nonstick cooking spray.

2. Pour cake mix into large bowl; stir in melted butter until well blended. Remove ½ cup dough and set aside. Press remaining dough evenly into prepared pan. Spread preserves evenly over dough in pan.

3. Place chips in medium bowl. Stir in reserved dough until well mixed. (Dough will remain in small lumps evenly distributed throughout chips.) Sprinkle mixture evenly over preserves.

4. Bake 20 minutes or until lightly browned and bubbly at edges. Cool completely in pan on wire rack.                    *Makes 3 dozen bars*

# sweet walnut maple bars

**Crust**

    **1 package DUNCAN HINES® Moist Deluxe® Classic Yellow Cake Mix, divided**

    **⅓ cup butter or margarine, melted**

    **1 egg**

**Topping**

    **1⅓ cups MRS. BUTTERWORTH'S® Maple Syrup**

    **3 eggs**

    **⅓ cup firmly packed light brown sugar**

    **½ teaspoon maple flavoring or vanilla extract**

    **1 cup chopped walnuts**

1. Preheat oven to 350°F. Grease 13×9×2-inch pan.

2. For crust, reserve ⅔ cup cake mix; set aside. Combine remaining cake mix, melted butter and egg in large bowl. Stir until thoroughly blended. (Mixture will be crumbly.) Press into prepared pan. Bake at 350°F for 15 to 20 minutes or until light golden brown.

3. For topping, combine reserved cake mix, maple syrup, eggs, brown sugar and maple flavoring in large bowl. Beat at low speed with electric mixer for 3 minutes. Pour over crust. Sprinkle with walnuts. Bake at 350°F for 30 to 35 minutes or until filling is set. Cool completely. Cut into bars. Store leftover bars in refrigerator.  *Makes 24 bars*

# buried cherry bars

1 jar (10 ounces) maraschino cherries
1 package (about 18 ounces) devil's food cake mix *without* pudding
    in the mix
1 cup (2 sticks) butter, melted
1 egg
½ teaspoon almond extract
1½ cups semisweet chocolate chips
¾ cup sweetened condensed milk
½ cup chopped pecans

1. Preheat oven to 350°F. Lightly grease 13×9-inch baking pan. Drain maraschino cherries, reserving 2 tablespoons juice. Cut cherries into quarters.

2. Combine cake mix, butter, egg and almond extract in large bowl; mix well. (Batter will be very thick.) Spread batter in prepared pan. Lightly press cherries into batter.

3. Combine chocolate chips and sweetened condensed milk in small saucepan. Cook over low heat, stirring constantly, until chocolate melts. Stir in reserved cherry juice. Spread chocolate mixture over cherries in pan; sprinkle with pecans.

4. Bake 35 minutes or until almost set in center. Cool completely in pan on wire rack. Cut into triangles or squares. *Makes 2 dozen bars*

# granola raisin bars

1 package (about 18 ounces) yellow cake mix with pudding in the mix,
  divided
½ cup (1 stick) butter, melted, divided
1 egg
4 cups granola cereal with raisins

1. Preheat oven to 350°F. Lightly spray 13×9-inch baking pan with nonstick cooking spray. Reserve ½ cup cake mix; set aside.

2. Combine remaining cake mix, ¼ cup melted butter and egg in large bowl; stir until well blended. (Dough will be thick and sticky.) Press dough evenly into prepared pan with plastic wrap. Bake 8 minutes.

3. Meanwhile, combine reserved cake mix, granola cereal and remaining ¼ cup melted butter in medium bowl; stir until well blended. Spread mixture evenly over partially baked bars.

4. Bake 15 to 20 minutes or until edges are lightly browned. Cool completely in pan on wire rack.                    *Makes 2½ dozen bars*

# easy turtle bars

1 package (about 18 ounces) chocolate cake mix
½ cup (1 stick) butter, melted
¼ cup milk
1 cup (6 ounces) semisweet chocolate chips
1 cup chopped pecans
1 jar (12 ounces) caramel ice cream topping

1. Preheat oven to 350°F. Spray 13×9-inch baking pan with nonstick cooking spray.

2. Combine cake mix, butter and milk in large bowl; stir until well blended. Press half of batter into prepared pan. Bake 7 to 8 minutes or until crust begins to form.

3. Sprinkle chocolate chips and half of pecans over partially baked crust. Drizzle with caramel topping. Drop spoonfuls of remaining batter over caramel mixture; sprinkle with remaining pecans.

4. Bake 18 to 20 minutes or until top springs back when lightly touched. (Caramel center will be soft.) Cool completely in pan on wire rack. Cut into bars. *Makes 2½ dozen bars*

# peanut butter cheesecake bars

1 package (about 18 ounces) yellow cake mix with pudding in the mix
½ cup (1 stick) butter, softened, cut into small pieces
2 packages (8 ounces each) cream cheese, softened
1 cup chunky peanut butter
3 eggs
1¼ cups sugar
1 cup salted roasted peanuts
Melted chocolate (optional)

1. Preheat oven to 325°F.

2. Beat cake mix and butter in medium bowl with electric mixer at medium speed just until crumbly. Reserve 1 cup dough. Press remaining dough evenly into ungreased 13×9-inch baking pan to form crust. Bake 10 minutes; cool on wire rack.

3. Beat cream cheese and peanut butter in large bowl with electric mixer at medium speed until fluffy. Beat in eggs, 1 at a time, scraping down side of bowl occasionally. Gradually beat in sugar until light. Spoon filling over cooled crust. Combine reserved dough and peanuts; sprinkle over filling.

4. Bake 45 minutes or until filling is just set and knife inserted into center comes out clean. Cool in pan on wire rack 30 minutes. Refrigerate at least 2 hours before serving. Drizzle with melted chocolate, if desired.

*Makes 2 to 3 dozen bars*

# lemon bars

1 package DUNCAN HINES® Moist Deluxe® Lemon Supreme Cake Mix
3 eggs, divided
⅓ cup butter-flavor shortening
½ cup granulated sugar
¼ cup lemon juice
2 teaspoons grated lemon peel
½ teaspoon baking powder
¼ teaspoon salt
   Confectioners' sugar

1. Preheat oven to 350°F.

2. Combine cake mix, 1 egg and shortening in large mixing bowl. Beat at low speed with electric mixer until crumbs form. Reserve 1 cup. Pat remaining mixture lightly into *ungreased* 13×9-inch pan. Bake at 350°F for 15 minutes or until lightly browned.

3. Combine remaining 2 eggs, granulated sugar, lemon juice, lemon peel, baking powder and salt in medium mixing bowl. Beat at medium speed with electric mixer until light and foamy. Pour over hot crust. Sprinkle with reserved crumb mixture.

4. Bake at 350°F for 15 minutes or until lightly browned. Sprinkle with confectioners' sugar. Cool in pan. Cut into bars.      *Makes 30 to 32 bars*

These bars are also delicious using Duncan Hines® Moist Deluxe® Classic Yellow Cake Mix.

# ice cream sandwiches

1 package (about 18 ounces) chocolate cake mix with pudding
    in the mix
2 eggs
¼ cup warm water
3 tablespoons butter, melted
2 cups vanilla ice cream, softened
    Colored sugars or sprinkles

1. Preheat oven to 350°F. Lightly spray 13×9-inch pan with nonstick cooking spray. Line pan with foil and spray foil.

2. Beat cake mix, eggs, water and melted butter in large bowl with electric mixer until well blended. (Dough will be thick and sticky.) Press dough evenly into prepared pan; prick surface with fork (about 40 times).

3. Bake 20 minutes or until toothpick inserted into center comes out clean. Cool in pan on wire rack.

4. Cut cookie in half crosswise; remove one half from pan. Spread ice cream evenly over cookie half remaining in pan. Top with second half; use foil in pan to wrap up sandwich.

5. Freeze at least 4 hours. Cut into 8 equal pieces; dip cut ends in sugar or sprinkles. Wrap sandwiches individually and freeze until ready to serve.

*Makes 8 sandwiches*

Peppermint Ice Cream Sandwiches: Stir ⅓ cup crushed peppermint candies into vanilla ice cream before assembling. Roll ends of sandwiches in additional crushed peppermint candies to coat.

Tip: If the ice cream is too hard to scoop easily, microwave on HIGH 10 seconds to soften.

# butterscotch blondies

1 (18.25-ounce) package yellow cake mix with pudding in the mix
⅓ cup butter or margarine, softened
3 eggs, divided
1 cup chopped pecans, toasted
1 cup (6 ounces) butterscotch-flavored chips
1 (14-ounce) can EAGLE BRAND® Sweetened Condensed Milk
  (NOT evaporated milk)
1 teaspoon vanilla extract

1. Preheat oven to 350°F. In large bowl, beat cake mix, butter and 1 egg with electric mixer at medium speed until crumbly.

2. Press evenly into greased 13×9-inch baking pan. Bake 15 minutes. Remove from oven; sprinkle with pecans and butterscotch chips.

3. In small bowl, beat EAGLE BRAND®, remaining 2 eggs and vanilla. Pour evenly over chips.

4. Bake 25 to 30 minutes longer or until center is set. Cool completely. Cut into bars. Store leftovers covered at room temperature.

*Makes 2 to 3 dozen bars*

# chocolate and oat toffee bars

¾ cup (1½ sticks) plus 2 tablespoons butter, softened, divided
1 package (about 18 ounces) yellow cake mix with pudding in the mix
2 cups uncooked quick oats
¼ cup packed brown sugar
1 egg
½ teaspoon vanilla
1 cup toffee baking bits
½ cup chopped pecans
⅓ cup semisweet chocolate chips

1. Preheat oven to 350°F. Grease 13×9-inch baking pan.

2. Beat ¾ cup butter in large bowl with electric mixer until creamy. Add cake mix, oats, brown sugar, egg and vanilla; beat 1 minute or until well blended. Stir in toffee bits and pecans. Pat dough into prepared pan.

3. Bake 31 to 35 minutes or until golden brown. Cool completely in pan on wire rack.

4. Melt remaining 2 tablespoons butter and chocolate chips in small saucepan over low heat. Drizzle warm glaze over bars. Let stand 1 hour at room temperature or until glaze is set. Cut into bars.

*Makes 2½ dozen bars*

# ooey-gooey caramel peanut butter bars

1 package (about 18 ounces) yellow cake mix *without* pudding
    in the mix
1 cup uncooked quick oats
⅔ cup creamy peanut butter
1 egg, slightly beaten
2 tablespoons milk
1 package (8 ounces) cream cheese, softened
1 jar (12¼ ounces) caramel ice cream topping
1 cup semisweet chocolate chips

1. Preheat oven to 350°F. Lightly grease 13×9-inch baking pan.

2. Combine cake mix and oats in large bowl. Cut in peanut butter
with pastry blender or two knives until mixture is crumbly.

3. Blend egg and milk in small bowl. Add to peanut butter mixture; stir
just until combined. Reserve 1½ cups mixture. Press remaining peanut
butter mixture into prepared pan.

4. Beat cream cheese in small bowl with electric mixer at medium speed
until fluffy. Add caramel topping; beat just until combined. Carefully spread
over peanut butter layer in pan. Break up reserved peanut butter mixture
into small pieces; sprinkle over cream cheese layer. Sprinkle with chocolate
chips.

5. Bake 30 minutes or until nearly set in center. Cool completely in pan on
wire rack. *Makes about 2½ dozen bars*

# pecan date bars

**Crust**

⅓ cup shortening plus additional for greasing

1 package DUNCAN HINES® Moist Deluxe® Classic White Cake Mix

1 egg

**Topping**

1 package (8 ounces) chopped dates

1¼ cups chopped pecans

1 cup water

½ teaspoon vanilla extract

Confectioners' sugar

1. Preheat oven to 350°F. Grease and flour 13×9-inch baking pan.

2. For crust, cut ⅓ cup shortening into cake mix with pastry blender or 2 knives until mixture resembles coarse crumbs. Add egg; stir well. (Mixture will be crumbly.) Press mixture into bottom of prepared pan.

3. For topping, combine dates, pecans and water in medium saucepan. Bring to a boil. Reduce heat; simmer until mixture thickens, stirring constantly. Remove from heat. Stir in vanilla extract. Spread date mixture evenly over crust. Bake at 350°F for 25 to 30 minutes. Cool completely. Dust with confectioners' sugar. *Makes about 32 bars*

# lemon cheese bars

1 package (about 18 ounces) white or yellow cake mix with pudding in the mix
2 eggs
⅓ cup vegetable oil
1 package (8 ounces) cream cheese, softened
⅓ cup sugar
1 teaspoon lemon juice

1. Preheat oven to 350°F.

2. Combine cake mix, 1 egg and oil in large bowl; stir until crumbly. Reserve 1 cup crumb mixture. Press remaining crumb mixture into ungreased 13×9-inch baking pan. Bake 15 minutes or until light golden brown.

3. Beat remaining egg, cream cheese, sugar and lemon juice in medium bowl with electric mixer at medium speed until smooth and well blended. Spread over baked crust. Sprinkle with reserved crumb mixture.

4. Bake 15 minutes or until cream cheese layer is just set. Cool in pan on wire rack. Cut into bars.                                        *Makes 2½ dozen bars*

To soften cream cheese quickly, remove it from the wrapper and place it on a microwavable plate. Microwave on MEDIUM (50%) 15 to 20 seconds or until slightly softened.

# chocolate macaroon squares

1 package (18.25 ounce) chocolate cake mix
⅓ cup butter or margarine, softened
1 large egg, lightly beaten
1 can (14 ounces) NESTLÉ® CARNATION® Sweetened Condensed Milk
1 egg
1 teaspoon vanilla extract
1⅓ cups flaked sweetened coconut, *divided*
1 cup chopped pecans
1 cup (6 ounces) NESTLÉ® TOLL HOUSE® Semi-Sweet Chocolate
    Morsels

**PREHEAT** oven to 350°F.

**COMBINE** cake mix, butter and egg in large bowl; mix with fork until crumbly. Press onto bottom of ungreased 13×9-inch baking pan. Combine sweetened condensed milk, egg and vanilla extract in medium bowl; beat until well blended. Stir in *1 cup* coconut, nuts and morsels.

**SPREAD** mixture evenly over base; sprinkle with *remaining* coconut. Bake for 28 to 30 minutes or until center is almost set (center will firm when cool). Cool in pan on wire rack.     *Makes 24 squares*

# banana gingerbread bars

1 package (14.5 ounces) gingerbread cake mix
½ cup lukewarm water
1 ripe, medium DOLE® Banana, mashed (about ½ cup)
1 egg
1 small DOLE® Banana, peeled and chopped
½ cup DOLE® Seedless Raisins
½ cup slivered almonds
1½ cups powdered sugar
   Juice from 1 lemon

• Preheat oven to 350°F.

• In large mixer bowl, combine gingerbread mix, water, mashed banana and egg. Beat on low speed of electric mixer 1 minute.

• Stir in chopped banana, raisins and almonds.

• Spread batter in greased 13×9-inch baking pan. Bake 20 to 25 minutes or until top springs back when lightly touched.

• In medium bowl, mix powdered sugar and 3 tablespoons lemon juice to make thin glaze. Spread over warm gingerbread. Cool before cutting into bars. Sprinkle with additional powdered sugar, if desired.

*Makes about 32 bars*

# red velvet brownies

    1 package (about 18 ounces) red velvet cake mix
 ¾ cup (1½ sticks) butter, softened
    2 eggs
1½ cup chopped pecans, divided
    1 container (16 ounces) cream cheese frosting
    Red sprinkles (optional)

1. Preheat oven 350°F. Line 13×9-inch baking pan with foil, leaving 1-inch overhang. Spray foil with nonstick cooking spray.

2. Beat cake mix, butter and eggs in large bowl with electric mixer at medium speed 1 minute. (Batter will be thick.) Add 1 cup pecans; beat 15 seconds or just until combined. Pour batter into prepared pan. Spray spatula with cooking spray; gently spread batter evenly in pan.

3. Bake 25 minutes or until toothpick inserted into center comes out almost clean. Cool completely in pan on wire rack.

4. Spread frosting over brownies; sprinkle with remaining ½ cup pecans and sprinkles, if desired. Refrigerate at least 2 hours before cutting. Store covered in refrigerator. *Makes 3 dozen brownies*

# orange coconut cream bars

1 (18¼-ounce) package yellow cake mix
1 cup quick-cooking or old-fashioned oats, uncooked
¾ cup chopped nuts
½ cup butter or margarine, melted
1 large egg
1 (14-ounce) can sweetened condensed milk
2 teaspoons grated orange zest
1 cup shredded coconut
1 cup "M&M's"® Semi-Sweet Chocolate Mini Baking Bits

Preheat oven to 375°F. Lightly grease 13×9×2-inch baking pan; set aside. In large bowl combine cake mix, oats, nuts, butter and egg until ingredients are thoroughly moistened and mixture resembles coarse crumbs. Reserve 1 cup mixture. Firmly press remaining mixture onto bottom of prepared pan; bake 10 minutes. In separate bowl combine condensed milk and orange zest; spread over baked base. Combine reserved crumb mixture, coconut and "M&M's"® Semi-Sweet Chocolate Mini Baking Bits; sprinkle evenly over condensed milk mixture and press in lightly. Continue baking 20 to 25 minutes or until golden brown. Cool completely. Cut into bars. Store in tightly covered container. *Makes 26 bars*

# triple chocolate cream cheese bars

1 package (about 18 ounces) chocolate cake mix
$\frac{1}{3}$ cup vegetable oil
3 eggs, divided
2 packages (8 ounces each) cream cheese, softened
$\frac{1}{3}$ cup sugar
1 cup sour cream
1 cup (6 ounces) semisweet chocolate chips, melted and cooled slightly
1 cup white chocolate chips

1. Preheat oven to 350°F. Grease 13×9-inch glass baking dish.

2. Combine cake mix, oil and 1 egg in medium bowl; mix well. Press onto bottom of prepared baking dish. Bake 10 minutes.

3. Meanwhile, beat cream cheese in large bowl with electric mixer at medium speed until light and fluffy. Add remaining 2 eggs and sugar; beat until well blended. Beat in sour cream and melted chocolate until blended. Pour mixture over partially baked crust; sprinkle with white chocolate chips.

4. Bake about 50 minutes or until set. Cool completely in pan on wire rack; refrigerate until chilled.                    *Makes 1½ dozen bars*

# Cool Kid
## Stuff

# miss pinky the pig cupcakes

2 jars (10 ounces each) maraschino cherries, well drained
1 package (about 18 ounces) white cake mix *without* pudding
   in the mix
1 cup sour cream
½ cup vegetable oil
3 egg whites
¼ cup water
½ teaspoon almond extract
1 container (16 ounces) cream cheese frosting
   Red food coloring
48 small gumdrops
   Mini candy-coated chocolate pieces, mini chocolate chips,
      white decorating icing and red sugar

**1.** Preheat oven to 350°F. Line 24 standard (2½-inch) muffin cups with paper baking cups. Spray 24 mini (1¾-inch) muffin cups with nonstick cooking spray. Pat cherries dry with paper towels. Place in food processor; process 4 to 5 seconds or until finely chopped.

**2.** Beat cake mix, sour cream, oil, egg whites, water and almond extract in large bowl with electric mixer at low speed 1 minute or until blended. Increase speed to medium; beat 1 to 2 minutes or until smooth. Stir in cherries.

**3.** Spoon about 2 slightly rounded tablespoons batter into each prepared standard muffin cup, filling about half full. (Cups will be slightly less full than normal.) Spoon remaining batter into prepared mini muffin cups, filling each about one-third full.

**4.** Bake standard cupcakes 14 to 18 minutes and mini cupcakes 7 to 9 minutes or until toothpick inserted into centers comes out clean. Cool cupcakes in pans 5 minutes. Remove from pans; cool completely on wire racks.

5. Blend frosting and food coloring in medium bowl until desired shade of pink is reached. Frost tops of standard cupcakes. Press top of mini cupcake onto one side of each standard cupcake top. Frost mini cupcakes.

6. Place gumdrops between two layers of waxed paper. Flatten to ⅛-inch thickness with rolling pin; cut out triangles. Arrange triangles on cupcakes for ears; decorate faces with chocolate pieces, chocolate chips, decorating icing and red sugar.                                    *Makes 24 cupcakes*

# flapjack party stack

1 package (about 18 ounces) yellow cake mix, plus ingredients to
    prepare mix
1 container (16 ounces) vanilla frosting
1 quart fresh strawberries, washed, hulled and sliced
1 cup caramel or butterscotch ice cream topping

1. Preheat oven to 350°F. Grease bottoms and sides of four 9-inch round cake pans; line pans with waxed paper.

2. Prepare and bake cake mix according to package directions, adjusting baking time as necessary. Cool cake layers in pans 15 minutes. Remove from pans; cool completely on wire racks.

3. Reserve ¼ cup frosting. Place one cake layer on serving plate; spread or pipe one third of remaining frosting in swirls on cake to resemble whipped butter. Top with one fourth of sliced strawberries. Repeat with next two cake layers, frosting and strawberries. Top stack with remaining cake layer.

4. Warm caramel topping in microwave just until pourable. Drizzle over cake. Spread or pipe reserved frosting in center; garnish with remaining strawberries.                                    *Makes 12 servings*

# slinky the snake

2 packages (about 18 ounces each) cake mix, any flavor, plus
    ingredients to prepare mix
2 containers (16 ounces each) white frosting
    Green food coloring
1 cup semisweet chocolate chips
    Red fruit roll-up
    Assorted candies

**1.** Prepare and bake cake mixes according to package directions for 12-cup bundt cakes. Cool completely.

**2.** Cut each bundt cake in half. Position each half end to end to form one long serpentine shape as shown in photo, attaching pieces with small amount of frosting.

**3.** Blend frosting and food coloring in large bowl until desired shade of green is reached. Frost entire length of cake with green frosting, spreading frosting about halfway down sides of cake.

**4.** Place chocolate chips in small resealable food storage bag. Microwave on HIGH 20 seconds. Knead bag several times; microwave at 10-second intervals until chocolate is melted. Cut off tiny corner of bag; pipe diamond pattern on back of snake.

**5.** Cut out tongue from fruit roll-up. Decorate face and back of snake with assorted candies. *Makes 32 to 36 servings*

# crayon craze

1 package (about 18 ounces) cake mix, any flavor, plus ingredients
   to prepare mix
2 containers (16 ounces each) white frosting
   Gold, green, red, yellow, orange and blue food coloring
4 flat-bottomed ice cream cones

1. Prepare and bake cake mix according to package directions for 13×9-inch cake. Cool completely.

2. Measure 4½ inches down long sides of cake; draw line across top of cake with toothpick to create 9×4½-inch rectangle. Using toothpick line as guide, carefully cut halfway through cake (about 1 inch). (Do *not* cut all the way through cake.)

3. Split cake horizontally from 9-inch side just to cut made at 4½-inch line. Remove 9×4½×1-inch piece of cake; discard. Round edges of 9-inch side to resemble top of crayon box.

4. Tint 1 container of frosting gold. Tint 1 cup frosting green. Divide remaining frosting into four parts (scant ¼ cup each). Tint one part red, one yellow, one orange and one blue. Frost entire cake with gold frosting. Using medium writing tip and green frosting, pipe "CRAYONS" on cake. Pipe stripes, triangles and decorative borders on crayon box.

5. Gently cut ice cream cones in half vertically with serrated knife. Frost each cone half different color (red, yellow, orange and blue). Place frosted cones on cake, just below rounded edge, to resemble crayon tips.

*Makes 16 to 18 servings*

# doodle bug cupcakes

1 package (about 18 ounces) white cake mix *without* pudding
   in the mix
1 cup sour cream
3 eggs
⅓ cup water
⅓ cup vegetable oil
1 teaspoon vanilla
1½ cups prepared cream cheese frosting
   Red, yellow, blue and green food coloring
   Red licorice strings, cut into 2-inch pieces
   Assorted round decorating candies

1. Preheat oven to 350°F. Line 24 standard (2½-inch) muffin cups with paper baking cups.

2. Beat cake mix, sour cream, eggs, water, oil and vanilla in large bowl with electric mixer at low speed 1 minute or until blended. Beat at medium speed 1 to 2 minutes or until smooth. Spoon batter into prepared muffin cups, filling about two-thirds full.

3. Bake 20 minutes or until toothpick inserted into centers comes out clean. Cool cupcakes in pans 5 minutes. Remove from pans; cool completely on wire racks.

4. Divide frosting evenly among four small bowls. Blend frosting and food coloring until desired shades are reached. Frost cupcakes.

5. Poke three small holes with toothpick, on opposite sides of each cupcake, making six holes total. Insert licorice piece into each hole for legs. Decorate tops of cupcakes with assorted candies.                *Makes 24 cupcakes*

# cookie pizza cake

1 package (about 16 ounces) refrigerated chocolate chip cookie dough
1 package (about 18 ounces) chocolate cake mix, plus ingredients
    to prepare mix
1 cup prepared vanilla frosting
½ cup peanut butter
1 to 2 tablespoons milk
1 container (16 ounces) chocolate frosting
  Chocolate peanut butter cups, chopped (optional)
  Peanut butter chips (optional)

1. Preheat oven to 350°F. Coat two 12-inch deep-dish pizza pans with nonstick cooking spray. Press cookie dough evenly into one pan. Bake 15 to 20 minutes or until edges are golden brown. Cool cookie in pan 20 minutes. Remove from pan; cool completely on wire rack.

2. Prepare cake mix according to package directions. Fill second pan one-fourth to half full with batter. (Reserve remaining cake batter for another use, such as cupcakes.) Bake 10 to 15 minutes or until toothpick inserted into center comes out clean. Cool cake in pan 15 minutes. Gently remove from pan; cool completely on wire rack.

3. Combine vanilla frosting and peanut butter in small bowl. Gradually stir in milk, 1 tablespoon at a time, until mixture is of spreadable consistency.

4. Place cookie on serving plate. Spread peanut butter frosting over cookie. Place cake on top of cookie, trimming cookie to match size of cake, if necessary. Frost top and side of cake with chocolate frosting. Garnish with peanut butter cups and peanut butter chips.

*Makes 12 to 14 servings*

# meteorite mini cakes

1 package (about 18 ounces) chocolate cake mix, plus ingredients
    to prepare mix
2 containers (16 ounces each) vanilla frosting, divided
    Assorted food coloring
1 bag (11 ounces) chocolate chunks

1. Preheat oven to 350°F. Spray 18 standard (2½-inch) muffin cups with nonstick cooking spray.

2. Prepare cake mix according to package directions. Divide batter evenly among muffin cups. Bake 20 to 25 minutes or until toothpick inserted into centers comes out clean. Cool cupcakes in pan 5 minutes. Remove from pan; cool completely on wire rack.

3. Use kitchen shears to trim cupcake edges and form rounded, irregular shapes. Place 2 cups frosting in medium microwavable bowl. Microwave on LOW (30%) about 30 seconds or until melted. Blend frosting and food coloring until desired shades are reached. Drizzle frosting over cupcakes, coating completely.

4. Chill cakes 20 minutes. Press chocolate chunks into cakes to create bumpy surface. Melt remaining frosting and tint as desired. Drizzle over cakes to coat baking chunks with frosting. Chill until ready to serve.

*Makes 18 mini cakes*

# pb & j sandwich cake

1 package (about 18 ounces) white cake mix, plus ingredients
    to prepare mix
¾ cup powdered sugar
5 tablespoons peanut butter
2 to 3 tablespoons whipping cream or milk
1 tablespoon butter, softened
½ cup strawberry or grape jam

1. Preheat oven to 350°F. Grease two 8-inch square baking pans.

2. Prepare cake mix according to package directions. Spread batter evenly in prepared pans.

3. Bake 30 minutes or until toothpick inserted into centers comes out clean. Cool cake layers in pans 30 minutes. Remove from pans; cool completely on wire racks.

4. Carefully slice off browned tops of both layers to create flat, even layers. Place one layer on serving plate, cut side up.

5. Beat powdered sugar, peanut butter, 2 tablespoons cream and butter with electric mixer at medium speed until light and creamy. Add remaining 1 tablespoon cream, if necessary, to reach spreading consistency. Gently spread filling over cut side of cake layer on serving plate. Spread jam over peanut butter filling. Top with second cake layer, cut side up.

6. Cut cake in half diagonally to resemble sandwich. To serve, cut into thin slices across the diagonal using serrated knife. *Makes 12 servings*

# sherbet starburst

1 package (about 18 ounces) lemon cake mix, plus ingredients
    to prepare mix
2 quarts raspberry or mango sherbet, or any flavors
1 container (15 ounces) white pourable frosting
    Yellow food coloring
    Orange decorating sugar

1. Prepare and bake cake mix according to package directions for two
8- or 9-inch round cake layers. Cool cake layers completely.

2. Scoop sherbet into small bowl. Freeze until ready to serve.

3. Cut one cake layer into 8 wedges. (Reserve remaining cake layer for
another use.) Place cake wedges on wire rack set over waxed paper-lined
baking sheet to catch drips.

4. Blend frosting and food coloring in medium microwavable bowl until
desired shade of yellow is reached. Microwave on HIGH 20 seconds; stir.
Pour frosting slowly over each cake wedge, making sure to cover all sides.
Sprinkle with sugar. Let stand about 20 minutes or until set.

5. When ready to serve, arrange cakes wedges in circle with tips pointing
out. Place bowl of sherbet in center. *Makes 8 servings*

# colossal birthday cupcake

1 package (about 18 ounces) devil's food cake mix, plus ingredients
   to prepare mix
1 container (16 ounces) vanilla or chocolate frosting, divided
¼ cup peanut butter
   Construction paper or aluminum foil
   Fruit-flavored candy wafers or chocolate shavings

1. Preheat oven to 350°F. Grease and flour two 8-inch round cake pans.

2. Prepare cake mix according to package directions. Spread batter evenly
in prepared pans. Bake 30 minutes or until toothpick inserted into centers
comes out clean. Cool cake layers completely.

3. Blend ¾ cup frosting and peanut butter in medium bowl. Place one cake
layer on serving plate; spread evenly with peanut butter frosting. Top with
second cake layer; spread top with remaining vanilla frosting, mounding
frosting slightly higher in center.

4. Cut 36×3½-inch piece of construction paper; pleat paper every ½ inch.
Wrap around side of cake to resemble baking cup. Arrange candy wafers
decoratively on frosting.                              *Makes 12 servings*

# touchdown!

1 package (about 18 ounces) cake mix, any flavor, plus ingredients
    to prepare mix
2 cups prepared white frosting
    Green food coloring
    Assorted color decorating gels
1 square (2 ounces) almond bark
2 pretzel rods
4 thin pretzel sticks
    Small bear-shaped graham cookies

**1.** Prepare and bake cake mix according to package directions for 13×9-inch cake. Cool completely.

**2.** Blend frosting and food coloring in medium bowl until desired shade of green is reached. Frost entire cake with green frosting. Pipe field lines with white decorating gel.

**3.** Melt almond bark in tall glass according to package directions. Break off one fourth of each pretzel rod; discard shorter pieces. Break 2 pretzel sticks in half. Dip pretzels in melted almond bark, turning to coat completely and tapping off excess. Using pretzel rods for support posts, pretzel sticks for crossbars and pretzel stick halves for uprights, arrange pretzels in two goalpost formations on waxed paper; let stand until set. Carefully peel waxed paper from goalposts; arrange on each end of cake.

**4.** Meanwhile, decorate bear-shaped cookies with decorating gels; arrange cookies on cake as desired.                    *Makes 16 to 20 servings*

# big purple purse

1 package (about 18 ounces) cake mix, any flavor, plus ingredients
    to prepare mix
1 container (16 ounces) white frosting
    Red and blue food coloring
2 red licorice pull-apart twists
1 white chocolate-coated pretzel
    Round sugar-covered colored candies
    Candy lipstick, necklace and ring (optional)
    Chocolate coins (optional)

1. Prepare and bake cake mix according to package directions for two
9-inch round cake layers. Cool cake layers in pans 10 minutes. Remove
from pans; cool completely on wire racks. Reserve one cake layer for
another use.

2. Blend frosting, 4 drops red food coloring and 4 drops blue food coloring
in medium bowl. Add additional food coloring, one drop at a time, until
desired shade of purple is reached.

3. Spread about ½ cup frosting over top of cake layer. Cut in half; press
frosted sides together to form half circle. Place cake, cut side down, on
serving plate.

4. Spread frosting over top and sides of cake. Press licorice twists into top
of cake to form purse handles. Add pretzel for clasp. Gently press round
candies into sides of cake. Arrange candy lipstick, necklace, ring and coins
around cake, if desired.                    *Makes 8 to 10 servings*

# pupcakes

1 package (about 18 ounces) chocolate cake mix, plus ingredients
    to prepare mix
½ cup (1 stick) butter, softened
4 cups powdered sugar
¼ to ½ cup half-and-half or milk
    Red and yellow fruit roll-ups
    Candy-coated chocolate pieces
    Assorted colored jelly beans

1. Preheat oven to 350°F. Line 24 standard (2½-inch) muffin cups with paper baking cups.

2. Prepare cake mix and bake in prepared pans according to package directions. Cool cupcakes in pans 15 minutes. Remove from pans; cool completely on wire racks.

3. Beat butter in large bowl with electric mixer until creamy. Gradually add powdered sugar to form very stiff frosting, scraping down side of bowl occasionally. Gradually add half-and-half until frosting is of desired consistency. Frost tops of cupcakes.

4. Cut out ear and tongue shapes from fruit roll-ups with scissors; arrange on cupcakes, pressing into frosting. Add chocolate pieces and jelly beans to create eyes and noses. *Makes 24 cupcakes*

# ladybug

1 package (about 18 ounces) white cake mix, plus ingredients
    to prepare mix

1 container (16 ounces) vanilla frosting

¼ cup red raspberry preserves

    Red decorating sugar

    Candy-coated chocolate pieces

8 dark chocolate discs or mint chocolate cookies

    String licorice and assorted gumdrops

    Large peppermint patty

2 cups shredded coconut tinted green with food coloring

1. Prepare and bake cake mix according to package directions for two 9-inch round cake layers. Cool cake layers completely.

2. Place one cake layer on serving plate; spread with frosting. Spread raspberry preserves over frosting to within ½ inch of edge. Top with second cake layer; frost top and side of cake with remaining frosting.

3. Sprinkle top of cake with sugar. Decorate with chocolate pieces and discs as shown in photo. Create ladybug face with string licorice and assorted gumdrops; attach to mint patty with small amounts of frosting. Place mint patty on cake. Press coconut onto side of cake.

*Makes 12 servings*

# pizza cake

1 package (about 18 ounces) yellow cake mix, plus ingredients
    to prepare mix
1 container (16 ounces) white frosting
    Red food coloring
    Orange round gummy candies
    Green sugar-coated sour gummy strips, cut into small pieces
    Purple round sour gummy rings
    White candy-coated licorice strips

1. Preheat oven to 350°F. Grease and flour 12-inch deep-dish pizza pan.

2. Prepare cake mix according to package directions. Pour batter into prepared pan.

3. Bake 18 to 25 minutes or until toothpick inserted into center comes out clean. Cool cake in pan 15 minutes. Remove from pan; cool completely on wire rack.

4. Blend frosting and food coloring in medium bowl until desired shade of red is reached. Place cake on serving plate; frost top of cake to within ¼ inch of edge.

5. Arrange candies over cake to resemble pizza toppings and cheese.

*Makes 12 servings*

# kitty kat

1 package (about 18 ounces) carrot cake mix, plus ingredients
    to prepare mix
1 container (16 ounces) cream cheese frosting
    Red and yellow food coloring
2 homemade or purchased cupcakes
¼ cup chocolate sprinkles
    Assorted round and heart-shape candies
    Black licorice string
    Candles

1. Preheat oven to 350°F. Prepare and bake cake mix according to package directions for two 8- or 9-inch round cake layers. Cool completely before frosting.

2. Blend frosting and food coloring in medium bowl until desired shade of orange is reached. Place one cake layer on serving plate; spread with frosting. Top with second cake layer; frost top and side of cake.

3. Cut ⅜ inch from 3 sides of each cupcake to create triangles for ears. Arrange triangles next to cake and frost. Scatter sprinkles around top edge of cake and in center of ears.

4. Decorate cat face with assorted candies. Cut licorice strings into 2-inch lengths for mouth. Arrange candles on cake to resemble whiskers.

*Makes 12 servings*

# beautiful butterflies

1 package (about 18 ounces) spice cake mix, plus ingredients
    to prepare mix
1 container (16 ounces) cream cheese or white chocolate frosting
    Food coloring
8 to 10 round chocolate wafer cookies, cut in half
    Pastel-colored candy-coated chocolate pieces
    Confetti sprinkles
    Decorating sugar (optional)

**1.** Preheat oven to 350°F. Grease and flour two 8-inch round cake pans.

**2.** Prepare cake mix according to package directions. Pour batter into prepared pans. Bake 30 minutes or until toothpick inserted into centers comes out clean. Cool cake layers in pans 10 minutes. Remove from pans; cool completely on wire racks.

**3.** Blend frosting and food coloring in medium bowl until desired shade is reached. Place one cake layer on serving plate; spread with ½ cup frosting. Top with second cake layer; frost top and side of cake.

**4.** Arrange two wafer cookie halves on cake about ½ inch apart, cut sides facing out, to create butterfly. Repeat with remaining cookies. Place two chocolate pieces in center of each butterfly as shown in photo. Arrange sprinkles on each butterfly to resemble antennae. Press remaining chocolate pieces into base of cake. Sprinkle top of cake with sugar.

*Makes 12 servings*

# lollipop garden bouquet

1 package (about 18 ounces) carrot cake mix, plus ingredients
    to prepare mix
1 container (16 ounces) white frosting
    Green food coloring
½ cup crushed chocolate wafer cookies
    Round hard sweet and sour candies
20 hard candy rings
    Green fruit roll-ups
5 to 10 lollipops

1. Prepare and bake cake mix according to package directions for one 8-inch round cake layer and one 9-inch round cake layer. Cool completely before frosting.

2. Blend frosting and food coloring in medium bowl until desired shade of green is reached. Place 8-inch cake layer on serving plate; spread top and side with frosting. Top with 9-inch cake layer; frost top and side of cake.

3. Sprinkle top of cake with cookie crumbs, leaving 1-inch border around edge of cake. Arrange round candies around top edge of cake as shown in photo. Press candy rings into side of bottom cake layer.

4. Use scissors to cut fruit roll-ups into 2½-inch leaf shapes. Press leaves onto lollipop sticks; arrange lollipops in center of cake.

*Makes 12 servings*

# flower power

1 package (about 18 ounces) spice cake mix, plus ingredients
    to prepare mix
1 container (16 ounces) white frosting
  Food coloring
5 to 10 large marshmallows
  Colored sugar
1 cup multi-colored mini marshmallows

1. Preheat oven to 350°F. Grease and flour two 8- or 9-inch round cake pans.

2. Prepare cake mix according to package directions. Pour batter into prepared pans. Bake 30 minutes or until toothpick inserted into centers comes out clean. Cool cake layers in pans 10 minutes. Remove from pans; cool completely on wire racks.

3. Blend frosting and food coloring in medium bowl until desired shade is reached. Place one cake layer on serving plate; spread with frosting. Top with second cake layer; frost top and side of cake.

3. Cut each large marshmallow crosswise into 3 slices with clean scissors. Arrange five marshmallow slices in circular pattern on cake to create flower, pressing pieces lightly into frosting. Repeat with remaining marshmallow slices.

4. Sprinkle center of each flower with sugar. Press mini marshmallows into base of cake.                                          *Makes 12 servings*

# banana cake splits

1 package (about 18 ounces) yellow cake mix *without* pudding
    in the mix
1 package (4-serving size) banana instant pudding and pie filling mix
1 cup water
½ cup (1 stick) butter, softened
3 eggs
3 cups *each* strawberry, chocolate and vanilla ice cream
6 bananas, sliced
¾ cup hot fudge dessert topping
    Whipped cream, nuts and maraschino cherries (optional)

1. Preheat oven to 350°F. Spray 11×17-inch jelly-roll pan with nonstick cooking spray.

2. Beat cake mix, pudding mix, water and butter in large bowl with electric mixer at low speed 1 minute. Add eggs; beat at medium speed 2 minutes or until well blended and fluffy. Pour batter evenly into prepared pan.

3. Bake 20 minutes or until toothpick inserted into center comes out clean. Cool cake in pan 10 minutes. Invert onto wire rack; cool completely.

4. Cut cake in half lengthwise, then cut crosswise into 1½- to 2-inch-wide pieces to create about 24 "bananas."

5. For each serving, arrange 2 "bananas" on plate. Top with ¼ cup *each* strawberry, chocolate and vanilla ice cream and half of 1 sliced banana. Drizzle with 1 tablespoon hot fudge; garnish with whipped cream, nuts and cherry. *Makes 12 servings*

# happy clown face

1 package (about 18 ounces) white cake mix, plus ingredients
    to prepare mix
1 container (16 ounces) white frosting
    Food coloring
    Assorted gumdrops, gummy candies, colored licorice strings
    and other candies
1 party hat
    Candles

**1.** Prepare and bake cake mix according to package directions for two
8- or 9-inch round cake layers. Cool completely before frosting.

**2.** Blend frosting and food coloring in medium bowl until desired shade is
reached. Place one cake layer on serving plate; spread with frosting. Top
with second cake layer; frost top and side of cake.

**3.** Decorate face of clown with assorted candies. Arrange party hat and
candles on cake as desired. *Makes 12 servings*

# s'more snack cake

1 package (about 18 ounces) yellow cake mix, plus ingredients
   to prepare mix
1 cup chocolate chunks, divided
2½ cups bear-shaped graham crackers (honey or chocolate), divided
1½ cups mini marshmallows

1. Preheat oven to 350°F. Grease 13×9-inch baking pan.

2. Prepare cake mix according to package directions; stir in ½ cup chocolate chunks and 1 cup graham crackers. Spread batter in prepared pan.

3. Bake 30 minutes. Remove cake from oven; sprinkle with remaining ½ cup chocolate chunks and marshmallows. Arrange remaining 1½ cups graham crackers evenly over top of cake.

4. Return cake to oven; bake 8 minutes or until marshmallows are golden brown. Cool completely before cutting.           *Makes 24 servings*

Note: This cake is best served the day it is made.

# giant gift boxes

1 package (about 18 ounces) chocolate or vanilla cake mix, plus
   ingredients to prepare mix
1 container (16 ounces) white frosting
   Green and orange food coloring
   Yellow decorating icing
   Candy sprinkles

1. Prepare and bake cake mix according to package directions for two
8- or 9-inch square cake layers. Cool completely before frosting.

2. Blend half of frosting and green food coloring in medium bowl until
desired shade of green is reached. Repeat with remaining frosting and
orange food coloring.

3. Place one cake layer on serving plate; frost top and sides with green
frosting. Pipe stripe of icing on each side to resemble ribbon. Let frosting
set before adding second cake layer. Place second cake layer slightly
off-center and rotated 45 degrees from bottom layer as shown in photo.
Frost top and sides with orange frosting. Pipe stripe of icing on each side
to resemble ribbon.

4. Pipe additional icing on top of cake for bow and streamers as shown in
photo. Decorate cake with sprinkles.                     *Makes 12 servings*

# flutter away

1 package (about 18 ounces) white or chocolate cake mix, plus ingredients to prepare mix
1 container (16 ounces) vanilla frosting
  Food coloring
1 filled rolled wafer cookie
  Gumdrops, gummy hearts and small round candies

1. Preheat oven to 350°F. Grease and flour two 9-inch round cake pans.

2. Prepare cake mix according to package directions. Pour batter into prepared pans. Bake 28 to 31 minutes or until toothpick inserted into centers comes out clean. Cool cake layers in pans 10 minutes. Remove from pans; cool completely on wire racks.

3. Blend frosting and food coloring in medium bowl until desired shade is reached. Cut each cake layer in half; place two halves on serving plate, cut sides facing out. Frost top of cake layers; top each half with remaining halves. Using serrated knife, cut small triangle out of each side of cake to form butterfly wings as shown in photo.

4. Frost top and sides of cake with remaining frosting. Place wafer cookie between cake halves to form butterfly body. Decorate wings with candies as desired. *Makes 12 servings*

# slam dunk

1 package (about 18 ounces) dark chocolate cake mix, plus
  ingredients to prepare mix
¾ cup crushed chocolate sandwich cookies (8 to 10 cookies)
1 container (16 ounces) dark chocolate frosting
1 cup prepared vanilla frosting
  Red and yellow food coloring
  Brown mini candy-coated chocolate pieces
  Orange candy-coated chocolate pieces

1. Prepare and bake cake mix according to package directions for two
9-inch round cake layers. Cool completely before frosting.

2. Place one cake layer on serving plate; spread with chocolate frosting.
Sprinkle crushed cookie crumbs over frosting. Top with second cake layer.
Frost side of cake with chocolate frosting, being careful not to get frosting
on top of cake.

3. Blend vanilla frosting and several drops of red and yellow food coloring
in small bowl until desired shade of orange is reached. Spread over top of
cake. Gently press meat mallet into frosting to create texture of basketball.
Arrange brown chocolate pieces on cake as shown in photo. Press orange
chocolate pieces into base of cake.                    *Makes 12 servings*

# Fun & Fruity

# crunchy peach snack cake

1 package (9 ounces) yellow cake mix
1 container (6 ounces) peach yogurt
1 egg
¼ cup peach fruit spread
¾ cup square whole grain oat cereal with cinnamon, slightly crushed
Whipped cream (optional)

1. Place rack in center of oven; preheat oven to 350°F. Lightly grease 8-inch square baking pan.

2. Beat cake mix, yogurt and egg in medium bowl with electric mixer at low speed 1 minute or until blended. Beat at medium speed 1 to 2 minutes or until smooth.

3. Spread batter in prepared pan. Drop fruit spread by ½ teaspoonfuls over cake batter. Sprinkle with cereal.

4. Bake 25 minutes or until toothpick inserted into center of cake comes out clean. Cool on wire rack. Serve with whipped cream, if desired.

*Makes 9 servings*

# double berry layer cake

1 package DUNCAN HINES® Moist Deluxe® Strawberry Supreme Cake Mix
⅔ cup strawberry jam
2½ cups fresh blueberries, rinsed, drained
1 container (8 ounces) frozen whipped topping, thawed
Fresh strawberry slices for garnish

1. Preheat oven to 350°F. Grease and flour two 9-inch round cake pans.

2. Prepare, bake and cool cakes following package directions for basic recipe.

3. Place one cake layer on serving plate. Spread with ⅓ cup strawberry jam. Arrange 1 cup blueberries on jam. Spread half the whipped topping to within ½ inch of cake edge. Place second cake layer on top. Repeat with remaining ⅓ cup strawberry jam, 1 cup blueberries and remaining whipped topping. Garnish with strawberry slices and remaining ½ cup blueberries. Refrigerate until ready to serve. *Makes 12 servings*

Tip: For best results, cut cake with serrated knife; clean knife after each slice.

## blueberry cream cheese pound cake

1 package (about 16 ounces) pound cake mix, divided
1½ cups fresh blueberries
4 ounces cream cheese, softened
2 eggs
¾ cup milk
Powdered sugar (optional)

1. Preheat oven to 350°F. Grease 9×5-inch loaf pan.

2. Place ¼ cup cake mix in medium bowl; add blueberries and toss until well coated.

3. Beat cream cheese in large bowl with electric mixer at medium speed 1 minute or until light and fluffy. Add eggs, 1 at a time, beating well after each addition.

4. Add remaining cake mix alternately with milk, beginning and ending with cake mix, beating well after each addition. Beat at medium speed 1 minute or until light and fluffy. Fold blueberry mixture into batter. Pour batter into prepared pan.

5. Bake 55 to 60 minutes or until toothpick inserted into center comes out clean. Cool cake in pan 10 minutes. Remove from pan; cool completely on wire rack. Lightly sprinkle with powdered sugar, if desired.

*Makes 12 servings*

# cran-lemon coffee cake

1 package (about 18 ounces) yellow cake mix with pudding in the mix
1 cup water
3 eggs
⅓ cup butter, melted and cooled
¼ cup fresh lemon juice
1 tablespoon grated lemon peel
1½ cups coarsely chopped cranberries
    Lemon Glaze (recipe follows)
    Additional grated lemon peel (optional)

1. Preheat oven to 350°F. Grease and flour 12-cup bundt pan.

2. Beat cake mix, water, eggs, butter, lemon juice and 1 tablespoon lemon peel in large bowl with electric mixer at low speed 2 minutes. Fold in cranberries. Spread batter evenly in prepared pan.

3. Bake 55 minutes or until toothpick inserted near center comes out clean. Cool in pan 15 minutes. Invert onto wire rack; cool completely.

4. Prepare Lemon Glaze; drizzle over coffee cake. Garnish with grated lemon peel. Serve warm or at room temperature.  *Makes 12 servings*

Lemon Glaze: Beat 1 cup powdered sugar and 3 tablespoons fresh lemon juice in small bowl until well blended.

Variation: For mini coffee cakes, grease and flour 9 mini (1-cup) bundt pan cups. Prepare batter as directed above; fill prepared cups almost two-thirds full. Bake 18 to 20 minutes or until toothpick inserted near centers comes out clean. Glaze and garnish as directed above.

# fresh fruit tart

1 package (about 18 ounces) butter recipe yellow cake mix
½ cup (1 stick) butter, melted and cooled
2 eggs
1 teaspoon vanilla
⅓ cup apricot jam
1½ cups thawed frozen whipped topping
2 cups sliced strawberries
1 kiwi, peeled and sliced
⅓ cup blueberries

1. Preheat oven to 350°F. Spray 10-inch springform pan with nonstick cooking spray.

2. Beat cake mix, butter, eggs and vanilla in large bowl with electric mixer at low speed 2 minutes. (Batter will be very thick.) Pour batter into prepared pan. Spray fingers with cooking spray and pat down top of batter to flatten slightly.

3. Bake 25 to 30 minutes or until center is firm and toothpick inserted into center comes out clean. Cool completely in pan on wire rack. Remove side of pan; slide cake onto serving platter.

4. Place apricot jam in small microwavable bowl. Microwave on HIGH 30 seconds or until jam is thin and syrupy.

5. Spread whipped topping evenly over crust. Arrange fruit decoratively over topping. Brush fruit with melted jam. Refrigerate leftovers.

*Makes 10 servings*

# apple spice custard cake

1 (18.25- or 18.5-ounce) package spice cake mix
2 medium apples, peeled, cored and chopped
1 (14-ounce) can EAGLE BRAND® Sweetened Condensed Milk
    (NOT evaporated milk)
1 (8-ounce) container sour cream
¼ cup lemon juice
    Ground cinnamon (optional)

1. Preheat oven to 350°F. Grease and flour 13×9-inch baking pan. Prepare cake mix according to package directions.

2. Stir in apples. Pour batter into prepared pan. Bake 30 to 35 minutes or until toothpick inserted near center comes out clean.

3. In medium bowl, combine EAGLE BRAND® and sour cream; mix well. Stir in lemon juice. Remove cake from oven; spread sour cream mixture evenly over hot cake.

4. Return to oven; bake 5 minutes or until set. Sprinkle with cinnamon (optional). Cool. Chill. Store leftovers covered in refrigerator.

*Makes 12 servings*

# pineapple almond coffee cake

1 can (8 ounces) crushed pineapple in juice, undrained
1 teaspoon cornstarch
1 tablespoon grated orange peel
1 package (9 ounces) yellow cake mix
⅓ cup water
1 egg
½ cup sliced almonds
1 tablespoon powdered sugar

1. Preheat oven to 350°F. Spray 9-inch springform pan with nonstick cooking spray.

2. Combine pineapple with juice and cornstarch in small saucepan; stir until smooth. Bring to a boil over medium-high heat; continue to boil 1 minute, stirring frequently. Remove from heat; stir in orange peel. Set aside to cool slightly.

3. Beat cake mix, water and egg in medium bowl with electric mixer at low speed 1 minute or until blended. Increase speed to medium; beat 1 to 2 minutes or until smooth. Pour half of batter into prepared pan. Spoon pineapple mixture evenly over batter. *Do not stir.* Gently spoon remaining batter evenly over pineapple mixture. Sprinkle with almonds.

4. Bake 30 minutes or until cake is golden and springs back when lightly pressed with fingertips. Remove to wire rack; cool completely. Remove side of pan; slide cake onto serving platter. Sprinkle with powdered sugar. Cut into wedges.                                    *Makes 10 servings*

Note: This cake will be puffy when it is removed from the oven, but will fall slightly upon cooling. The pineapple will settle to the bottom, making a slightly moist base.

# flower power strawberry cake

1 package (about 18 ounces) white cake mix *without* pudding
    in the mix
2 containers (6 ounces each) strawberry yogurt
4 eggs
1/3 cup vegetable oil
1 package (4-serving size) strawberry gelatin
1 container (8 ounces) thawed frozen whipped topping, divided
13 medium strawberries
    Yellow food coloring

1. Preheat oven to 350°F. Lightly grease 13×9-inch baking pan.

2. Beat cake mix, yogurt, eggs, oil and gelatin in large bowl with electric mixer at low speed 1 minute or until blended. Beat at medium speed 1 to 2 minutes or until smooth. Spread batter evenly in prepared pan.

3. Bake 38 to 43 minutes or until toothpick inserted into center comes out clean. Cool completely in pan on wire rack.

4. Reserve 1/2 cup whipped topping. Spread remaining topping over cake; score into 15 (3×2 1/2-inch) rectangles. Cut each strawberry lengthwise into 6 wedges. Place 5 strawberry wedges in each rectangle on cake, pointed ends towards center, making flower as shown in photo.

5. Blend reserved whipped topping and yellow food coloring in small bowl until desired shade of yellow is reached. Place in resealable food storage bag; cut off 1/8 inch from corner of bag. Pipe dot into center of each flower. Serve cake immediately or loosely cover and refrigerate for up to 24 hours.

*Makes 15 servings*

Fun & Fruity

# berry cobbler cake

2 cups (1 pint) fresh or frozen berries (blueberries, blackberries
    and/or raspberries)
1 package (9 ounces) yellow cake mix
1 teaspoon ground cinnamon
1 egg
1 cup water, divided
¼ cup sugar
1 tablespoon cornstarch
    Ice cream (optional)

1. Preheat oven to 375°F.

2. Place berries in 9-inch square baking pan; set aside.

3. Combine cake mix and cinnamon in large bowl. Add egg and ¼ cup water; stir until well blended. Spoon over berries.

4. Combine sugar and cornstarch in small bowl. Stir in remaining ¾ cup water until sugar mixture dissolves; pour over cake batter and berries.

5. Bake 40 to 45 minutes or until lightly browned. Serve warm or at room temperature with ice cream, if desired. *Makes 6 servings*

# apple-walnut glazed spice baby cakes

1 package (about 18 ounces) spice cake mix
1⅓ cups plus 3 tablespoons water, divided
3 eggs
⅓ cup vegetable oil
½ teaspoon vanilla
¾ cup chopped walnuts
12 ounces Granny Smith apples, peeled and cut into ½-inch cubes
(about 3 medium)
¼ teaspoon ground cinnamon
1 jar (12 ounces) caramel ice cream topping

1. Preheat oven to 350°F. Grease and flour 12 mini (1-cup) bundt pan cups.

2. Beat cake mix, 1⅓ cups water, eggs, oil and vanilla in large bowl with electric mixer at low speed 30 seconds. Beat at medium speed 2 minutes. Spoon batter evenly into prepared cups.

3. Bake 25 minutes or until toothpick inserted near centers comes out clean. Cool cakes in pans 15 minutes. Invert cakes onto wire racks; cool completely.

4. Meanwhile, place large skillet over medium-high heat. Add walnuts; cook and stir 3 minutes or until lightly browned. Transfer to small bowl. Combine apples, remaining 3 tablespoons water and cinnamon in same skillet; cook and stir over medium-high heat 3 minutes or until apples are crisp-tender. Remove from heat; stir in walnuts and caramel topping. Spoon apple mixture over cakes.                    *Makes 12 mini cakes*

# topsy-turvy banana crunch cake

⅓ cup uncooked old-fashioned oats
3 tablespoons packed brown sugar
1 tablespoon all-purpose flour
¼ teaspoon ground cinnamon
2 tablespoons butter
2 tablespoons chopped pecans
1 package (9 ounces) yellow cake mix
½ cup sour cream
½ cup mashed banana (about 1 medium)
1 egg, slightly beaten

1. Preheat oven to 350°F. Lightly grease 8-inch square baking pan.

2. Combine oats, brown sugar, flour and cinnamon in small bowl. Cut in butter with pastry blender or 2 knives until crumbly. Stir in pecans.

3. Beat cake mix, sour cream, banana and egg in medium bowl with electric mixer at low speed 1 minute or until blended. Beat at medium speed 1 to 2 minutes or until smooth. Spoon half of batter into prepared pan; sprinkle with half of oat topping. Top with remaining batter and topping.

4. Bake 25 to 30 minutes or until toothpick inserted into center comes out clean. Cool completely in pan on wire rack.           *Makes 9 servings*

# tropical sunshine cake

1 package (18.25 ounces) yellow cake mix
1 can (12 fluid ounces) NESTLÉ® CARNATION® Evaporated Milk
2 large eggs
1 can (20 ounces) crushed pineapple in juice, drained (juice reserved), *divided*
½ cup chopped almonds
¾ cup sifted powdered sugar
1 cup flaked coconut, toasted
   Whipped cream

**PREHEAT** oven to 350°F. Grease 13×9-inch baking pan.

**COMBINE** cake mix, evaporated milk and eggs in large mixer bowl. Beat on low speed for 2 minutes. Stir in *1 cup* pineapple. Pour batter into prepared baking pan. Sprinkle with almonds.

**BAKE** for 30 to 35 minutes or until wooden pick inserted in center comes out clean. Cool in pan on wire rack for 15 minutes.

**COMBINE** sugar and 2 tablespoons *reserved* pineapple juice in small bowl; mix until smooth. Spread over warm cake; sprinkle with coconut and *remaining* pineapple. Cool completely before serving. Top with whipped cream.                              *Makes 12 servings*

# mandarin orange tea cake

1 package (about 16 ounces) pound cake mix
½ cup plus 2 tablespoons orange juice, divided
2 eggs
¼ cup milk
1 can (15 ounces) mandarin orange segments in light syrup, drained
¾ cup powdered sugar
Grated peel of 1 orange

1. Preheat oven to 350°F. Grease 12-cup bundt pan.

2. Beat cake mix, ½ cup orange juice, eggs and milk in large bowl with electric mixer at medium speed 2 minutes or until light and fluffy. Fold in orange segments. Pour batter into prepared pan.

3. Bake 45 minutes or until golden brown and toothpick inserted near center comes out clean. Cool in pan 15 minutes. Invert cake onto wire rack; cool completely.

4. Combine powdered sugar, orange peel and remaining 2 tablespoons orange juice in small bowl; stir until smooth. Drizzle glaze over cake. Allow glaze to set about 5 minutes before serving. *Makes 16 servings*

# strawberry stripe refrigerator cake

**Cake**
>  1 package DUNCAN HINES® Moist Deluxe® Classic White Cake Mix
>  2 packages (10 ounces) frozen sweetened strawberry slices, thawed

**Topping**
>  1 package (4-serving size) vanilla-flavor instant pudding and
>    pie filling mix
>  1 cup milk
>  1 cup whipping cream, whipped
>    Fresh strawberries for garnish (optional)

1. Preheat oven to 350°F. Grease and flour 13×9×2-inch pan.

2. For cake, prepare, bake and cool following package directions. Poke holes 1 inch apart in top of cake using handle of wooden spoon. Purée thawed strawberries with juice in blender or food processor. Spoon evenly over top of cake, allowing mixture to soak into holes.

3. For topping, combine pudding mix and milk in large bowl. Stir until smooth. Fold in whipped cream. Spread over cake. Decorate with fresh strawberries, if desired. Refrigerate at least 4 hours.

*Makes 12 to 16 servings*

Variation: For a Neapolitan Refrigerator Cake, substitute Duncan Hines® Moist Deluxe® Devil's Food Cake Mix for White Cake Mix and follow directions listed above.

# easy apple butter cake

1 package (about 18 ounces) yellow cake mix *without* pudding
   in the mix
1 package (4-serving size) vanilla instant pudding and pie filling mix
4 eggs
1 cup sour cream
1 cup apple butter
½ cup apple juice
¼ cup vegetable oil
1 teaspoon ground cinnamon
½ teaspoon ground nutmeg
½ teaspoon ground cloves
¼ teaspoon salt
   Powdered sugar (optional)

1. Preheat oven to 375°F. Spray 10-inch tube pan with nonstick cooking spray.

2. Beat cake mix, pudding mix, eggs, sour cream, apple butter, apple juice, oil, cinnamon, nutmeg, cloves and salt in large bowl with electric mixer at low speed 1 minute. Beat at medium speed 2 minutes or until well blended and fluffy. Pour batter into prepared pan.

3. Bake 45 to 50 minutes or until toothpick inserted near center comes out clean. Cool cake in pan 20 minutes. Run sharp knife along edge of pan to release cake from pan; invert cake onto serving plate. Cool completely.

4. Just before serving, place 9-inch paper doily over cake; sift powdered sugar over doily. Carefully remove doily. *Makes 12 servings*

# caribbean cake squares

1 package (9 ounces) yellow cake mix
2 egg whites
½ cup orange juice
2 cans (8 ounces each) crushed pineapple in juice
  Additional orange juice
1 tablespoon cornstarch
½ cup slivered almonds
½ cup shredded coconut
2 large ripe bananas
1 can (15 ounces) mandarin orange segments in light syrup, drained

1. Preheat oven to 350°F. Spray 13×9-inch nonstick baking pan with nonstick cooking spray.

2. Beat cake mix, egg whites and orange juice in medium bowl with electric mixer at medium speed 2 minutes or until well blended. Spoon batter evenly into prepared pan.

3. Bake 11 to 12 minutes or until toothpick inserted into center comes out clean. Cool completely in pan on wire rack.

4. Drain pineapple juice into 2-cup measure; add additional orange juice to measure 1½ cups liquid. Stir in cornstarch until smooth. Pour juice mixture into medium saucepan. Bring to a boil over high heat, stirring constantly. Boil 1 minute, stirring constantly. Remove from heat.

5. Place almonds and coconut in large skillet; heat over medium heat until almonds and coconut are golden brown, stirring frequently.

6. Spread pineapple evenly over cake. Slice bananas and arrange over pineapple. Top with mandarin orange segments. Carefully drizzle juice mixture evenly over fruit. Sprinkle with almond mixture. Cover and refrigerate 1 to 4 hours. *Makes 16 servings*

# chocolate-raspberry layer cake

2 packages (about 18 ounces each) chocolate cake mix, plus
   ingredients to prepare mixes
1 jar (10 ounces) seedless red raspberry fruit spread
1 package (12 ounces) white chocolate chips, divided
1 container (16 ounces) chocolate frosting
½ pint fresh raspberries
1 to 2 cups sliced almonds, toasted*

*To toast almonds, spread in single layer on baking sheet. Bake in preheated
350°F oven 7 to 9 minutes or until golden brown, stirring frequently.

1. Preheat oven to 350°F. Grease and flour four 9-inch round cake pans.

2. Prepare and bake cake mixes according to package directions. Cool
cake layers in pans 15 minutes. Remove from pans; cool completely on
wire racks.

3. Place one cake layer on serving plate. Spread with one third of fruit
spread; sprinkle with ½ cup white chocolate chips. Repeat with second
and third cake layers, fruit spread and white chocolate chips.

4. Place fourth cake layer on top. Frost top and side of cake with chocolate
frosting. Decorate top of cake with concentric circles of raspberries and
remaining ½ cup white chocolate chips. Press almonds into frosting on
side of cake.                                    *Makes 12 to 16 servings*

# lemon-cherry coffee cake

½ cup (1 stick) cold butter, cut into pieces
2 packages (9 ounces each) single layer yellow cake mix
¼ cup buttermilk
1 egg
1 teaspoon vanilla
1 teaspoon grated lemon or orange peel
½ cup dried cherries or cranberries
1 egg white
½ teaspoon water
1 tablespoon sugar
½ cup sliced almonds

1. Preheat oven to 350°F. Spray 9-inch springform pan with nonstick cooking spray.

2. Cut butter into cake mix in large bowl with 2 knives or pastry blender until well blended. Stir in buttermilk, egg, vanilla and lemon peel until blended. Fold in dried cherries. (Batter will be sticky.)

3. Spoon batter into prepared pan; spread to edge of pan with moistened hands. Beat egg white and water in small bowl; brush over top of batter. Sprinkle with sugar. Score circle into 8 wedges with knife. Sprinkle with almonds.

4. Bake 20 to 25 minutes or until crust is golden brown and toothpick inserted into center comes out clean. Immediately cut into wedges along score lines. Cool in pan on wire rack 10 minutes. Remove side and base of pan. Serve warm.                    *Makes 8 servings*

# fruit-layered cheesecake squares

1 package (about 18 ounces) yellow cake mix
½ cup (1 stick) butter, softened
2 eggs
3 tablespoons water
2 packages (8 ounces each) cream cheese, softened
1 cup powdered sugar
¼ cup milk
2 teaspoons vanilla
1 can (8 ounces) pineapple tidbits, drained and juice reserved
3 tablespoons orange juice
¾ teaspoon cornstarch
1 medium banana (about 6 ounces), peeled and thinly sliced
1 cup fresh mango or nectarine pieces
1 pint whole strawberries, quartered

1. Preheat oven to 350°F. Grease 13×9-inch baking pan.

2. Beat cake mix, butter, eggs and water in large bowl with electric mixer at low speed 1 to 2 minutes or until stiff dough forms. Press dough evenly onto bottom of prepared pan. Bake 27 minutes or until toothpick inserted into center comes out clean. Cool completely in pan on wire rack.

3. Meanwhile, beat cream cheese, sugar, milk and vanilla in medium bowl with electric mixer at low speed 30 seconds or until just blended. Beat at high speed 1 minute or until smooth.

4. Blend reserved pineapple juice, orange juice and cornstarch in small saucepan until cornstarch is completely dissolved. Cook and stir over medium heat until mixture comes to a boil; cook and stir 1 minute. Remove from heat; set aside to cool completely.

5. Spread cream cheese frosting over crust; arrange fruit on top. Spoon or brush pineapple juice mixture over fruit. Cover with plastic wrap; refrigerate 1 hour or up to 1 day before serving.                    *Makes 16 servings*

# mango-orange pound cake

1 package (about 16 ounces) pound cake mix, plus ingredients
   to prepare mix
2 ripe mangoes, peeled and diced, divided
1 teaspoon grated orange peel
1½ cups powdered sugar
2 to 3 teaspoons orange juice
½ teaspoon vanilla
¼ teaspoon coconut extract (optional)

1. Preheat oven according to package directions. Grease and flour 9-cup nonstick bundt pan.

2. Prepare cake mix according to package instructions; stir in ½ cup mango and orange peel. Pour batter into prepared pan.

3. Bake 36 to 40 minutes or until toothpick inserted near center comes out clean. Cool cake in pan 10 minutes. Invert onto wire rack; cool completely.

4. Meanwhile, combine powdered sugar, 2 teaspoons orange juice, vanilla and coconut extract, if desired, in small bowl; stir until smooth. Add additional 1 teaspoon orange juice, if necessary, for pourable glaze.

5. Place cake on serving plate. Pour glaze evenly over cake, allowing it to drip down side of cake. Sprinkle remaining mango over cake.

*Makes 8 to 10 servings*

# taffy apple snack cake

1 package (about 18 ounces) yellow cake mix with pudding
   in the mix, divided
2 eggs
¼ cup water
¼ cup vegetable oil
4 tablespoons packed brown sugar, divided
2 medium apples, peeled and diced
1 cup chopped nuts (optional)
2 tablespoons butter, melted
¼ teaspoon ground cinnamon
½ cup caramel topping

1. Preheat oven to 350°F. Spray 8-inch square baking pan with nonstick cooking spray. Reserve ¾ cup cake mix in medium bowl.

2. Beat remaining cake mix, eggs, water, oil and 2 tablespoons brown sugar in large bowl with electric mixer at medium speed 2 minutes. Stir in apples. Spread batter in prepared pan.

3. Combine reserved cake mix, remaining 2 tablespoons brown sugar, nuts, if desired, butter and cinnamon in medium bowl; mix until well blended. Sprinkle over batter.

4. Bake 40 to 45 minutes or until toothpick inserted into center comes out clean. Cool completely in pan on wire rack. Cut into squares; top each serving with about 2 teaspoons caramel topping.     *Makes 9 servings*

# sweet and sour brunch cake

1 package (16 ounces) frozen rhubarb, thawed and patted dry
1 cup packed brown sugar
1 tablespoon all-purpose flour
1 teaspoon ground cinnamon
¼ cup (½ stick) butter, diced
1 package (about 18 ounces) yellow cake mix *without* pudding
    in the mix
1 package (4-serving size) vanilla instant pudding and pie filling mix
4 eggs
⅔ cup sour cream
½ cup water
½ cup vegetable oil

1. Preheat oven to 350°F. Spray 13×9-inch baking pan with nonstick cooking spray.

2. Spread rhubarb evenly in single layer in prepared pan. Combine brown sugar, flour and cinnamon in small bowl; mix well. Sprinkle over rhubarb; dot with butter.

3. Beat cake mix, pudding mix, eggs, sour cream, water and oil in large bowl with electric mixer at low speed 1 minute. Beat at medium speed 2 minutes or until well blended and creamy. Pour batter into prepared pan, spreading carefully over rhubarb mixture.

4. Bake 40 to 50 minutes or until toothpick inserted into center comes out clean. *Makes 16 to 18 servings*

Note: If frozen rhubarb is unavailable, substitute frozen unsweetened strawberries.

# blueberry angel food cake rolls

**1 package DUNCAN HINES® Angel Food Cake Mix**
**¼ cup confectioners' sugar plus additional for dusting towels**
**1 can (21 ounces) blueberry pie filling**
**Mint leaves for garnish (optional)**

1. Preheat oven to 350°F. Line two 15½×10½×1-inch jelly-roll pans with aluminum foil.

2. Prepare cake mix as directed on package. Divide and spread evenly into prepared pans. Cut through batter with knife or spatula to remove large air bubbles. Bake at 350°F for 15 minutes or until set. Invert cakes at once onto clean, lint-free dishtowels dusted with confectioners' sugar. Remove foil carefully. Roll up each cake with towel jelly-roll fashion, starting at short end. Cool completely.

3. Unroll cakes. Spread about 1 cup blueberry pie filling to within 1 inch of edges on each cake. Reroll and place seam-side down on serving plate. Dust with ¼ cup confectioners' sugar. Garnish with mint leaves, if desired.

*Makes 2 cakes (8 servings each)*

Tip: For a variation in flavor, substitute cherry pie filling for the blueberry pie filling.

# lemon-orange party cake

1 package (about 18 ounces) yellow cake mix with pudding in the mix
1¼ cups plus 5 tablespoons orange juice, divided
3 eggs
⅓ cup vegetable oil
2 tablespoons grated orange peel
5½ cups sifted powdered sugar, divided
⅓ cup lemon juice
⅓ cup butter, softened
    Colored sprinkles
20 candied lemon or orange slices

1. Preheat oven to 350°F. Lightly grease 13×9-inch baking pan.

2. Beat cake mix, 1¼ cups orange juice, eggs, oil and orange peel in large bowl with electric mixer at low speed 1 minute or until blended. Beat at medium speed 1 to 2 minutes or until smooth. Pour batter into prepared pan.

3. Bake 33 to 38 minutes or until toothpick inserted into center comes out clean. Meanwhile, combine 1 cup powdered sugar and lemon juice in small bowl; stir until smooth.

4. Pierce top of warm cake at ½-inch intervals with large fork or wooden skewer. Slowly drizzle lemon glaze over warm cake. Cool completely in pan on wire rack.

5. Beat remaining 4½ cups powdered sugar and butter in large bowl with electric mixer at low speed until blended. Beat in enough remaining orange juice to reach spreading consistency. Spread frosting over cake; decorate with sprinkles and candied lemon slices. *Makes 20 servings*

# delicious strawberry torte

4 eggs, separated
1 package (about 18 ounces) yellow cake mix
1 package (4-serving size) vanilla instant pudding and pie filling mix
1⅓ cups milk
¼ cup vegetable oil
1 teaspoon vanilla
Cream Cheese Icing (recipe follows)
1 quart strawberries, stemmed and halved
Whole strawberries (optional)

1. Preheat oven to 375°F. Grease and flour two 9-inch round cake pans.

2. Beat egg whites in medium bowl with electric mixer at high speed until soft peaks form. Beat cake mix, pudding mix, milk, egg yolks, oil and vanilla in large bowl at medium speed 2 minutes or until well blended. Fold in egg whites. Pour batter into prepared pans.

3. Bake 28 to 32 minutes or until toothpick inserted into centers comes out clean. Cool cake layers in pans 15 minutes. Remove from pans; cool completely on wire racks. Meanwhile, prepare Cream Cheese Icing.

4. Cut each cake layer in half horizontally. Place one cake layer on serving plate. Spread with icing; top with one third of strawberry halves. Repeat with second and third cake layers, icing and strawberry halves. Top with fourth cake layer; spread with icing. Garnish with whole strawberries.

*Makes 12 servings*

Cream Cheese Icing: Beat 1 package (8 ounces) softened cream cheese, 1 container (8 ounces) thawed frozen whipped topping, 1 cup granulated sugar, 1 cup powdered sugar, ¼ cup (½ stick) softened butter and 1 teaspoon vanilla in medium bowl with electric mixer until smooth. Refrigerate until ready to use.

# Chocolate

## *Obsession*

# tortoise snack cake

1 package (about 18 ounces) devil's food cake mix, plus ingredients
  to prepare mix
1 cup chopped pecans
1 cup semisweet chocolate chips
½ teaspoon vanilla
½ cup caramel sauce
  Additional caramel sauce and chopped pecans

**1.** Preheat oven to 350°F. Grease 13×9-inch baking pan.

**2.** Prepare cake mix according to package directions; stir in pecans, chocolate chips and vanilla. Pour batter into prepared pan. Drizzle ½ cup caramel sauce over batter; swirl caramel into batter with knife.

**3.** Bake 32 minutes or until cake begins to pull away from sides of pan and toothpick inserted into center comes out clean. Cool slightly in pan on wire rack. Top each serving with additional caramel sauce and pecans.

*Makes 24 servings*

# double chocolate chewies

1 package DUNCAN HINES® Moist Deluxe® Butter Recipe Fudge
  Cake Mix
2 eggs
½ cup (1 stick) butter or margarine, melted
1 package (6 ounces) semisweet chocolate chips
1 cup chopped nuts
  Confectioners' sugar (optional)

**1.** Preheat oven to 350°F. Grease bottom only of 13×9×2-inch baking pan.

**2.** Combine cake mix, eggs and melted butter in large bowl. Stir until thoroughly blended. (Mixture will be stiff.) Stir in chocolate chips and nuts.

Press mixture evenly into prepared pan. Bake at 350°F for 25 to 30 minutes or until toothpick inserted in center comes out clean. *Do not overbake.* Cool completely. Cut into bars. Dust with confectioners' sugar, if desired.

*Makes 36 bars*

Tip: For a special effect, cut a paper towel into ¼-inch-wide strips. Place strips in diagonal pattern on top of cooled bars before cutting. Place confectioners' sugar in tea strainer. Tap strainer lightly to dust surface with sugar. Carefully remove strips.

## double chocolate bundt cake

1 package (about 18 ounces) chocolate cake mix *without* pudding in the mix
1 package (4-serving size) chocolate instant pudding and pie filling mix
4 eggs, beaten
¾ cup water
¾ cup sour cream
½ cup oil
1 cup semisweet chocolate chips
Powdered sugar

1. Preheat oven to 350°F. Spray 12-cup bundt or tube pan with nonstick cooking spray.

2. Beat cake mix, pudding mix, eggs, water, sour cream and oil in large bowl with electric mixer at medium speed until well blended. Stir in chocolate chips; pour into prepared pan.

3. Bake 55 to 60 minutes or until cake springs back when lightly touched. Cool cake in pan 1 hour. Invert cake onto serving plate; cool completely. Sprinkle with powdered sugar before serving.     *Makes 10 to 12 servings*

# chocolate gingersnaps

¾ cup sugar
1 package (about 18 ounces) chocolate cake mix *without* pudding
  in the mix
1 tablespoon ground ginger
2 eggs
⅓ cup vegetable oil

**1.** Preheat oven to 350°F. Spray cookie sheets with nonstick cooking spray. Place sugar in shallow bowl.

**2.** Combine cake mix and ginger in large bowl. Add eggs and oil; stir until well blended. Shape tablespoonfuls of dough into 1-inch balls; roll in sugar to coat. Place 2 inches apart on prepared cookie sheets.

**3.** Bake 10 minutes or until set and tops are beginning to crack. Remove cookies to wire racks to cool completely.

*Makes about 3 dozen cookies*

Purchase ground ginger in small amounts, as it will begin to lose its flavor after four to six months. Like other spices, it should be stored in an airtight container in a cool, dry place.

# white chocolate lovers' layer cake

12 squares (1 ounce each) white chocolate, divided
1 cup (2 sticks) butter, softened, divided
1 package (about 18 ounces) white cake mix
1 cup milk
3 eggs
1½ teaspoons vanilla, divided
6 ounces cream cheese, softened
Dash salt
1½ cups powdered sugar
¼ cup seedless raspberry jam
1 cup fresh raspberries (optional)

1. Preheat oven to 350°F. Grease and flour two 9-inch round cake pans. Microwave 6 squares white chocolate and ½ cup butter in microwavable bowl on MEDIUM-HIGH (70%) 1½ minutes; stir. If necessary, microwave at additional 10- to 15-second intervals, stirring just until chocolate is melted. Cool slightly.

2. Beat cake mix, milk, eggs, ¾ teaspoon vanilla and white chocolate mixture in large bowl with electric mixer at low speed 1 minute. Beat at medium speed 2 minutes or until well blended. Pour into prepared pans.

3. Bake 25 minutes or until toothpick inserted into centers comes out clean. Cool cake layers in pans 10 minutes. Remove from pans; cool completely on wire racks.

4. Melt remaining 6 squares white chocolate; cool slightly. Beat remaining ½ cup butter and cream cheese in medium bowl with electric mixer until well blended. Beat in melted chocolate, remaining ¾ teaspoon vanilla and salt. Add powdered sugar; beat until frosting is light and fluffy.

5. Place one cake layer on serving plate. Top with frosting; spread jam evenly over frosting. Place second cake layer over jam. Frost top and side of cake with remaining frosting. Garnish with raspberries. *Makes 12 servings*

# triple chocolate pb minis

2 packages (4.4 ounces each) chocolate peanut butter cups*
1 package (about 18 ounces) chocolate fudge cake mix, plus
    ingredients to prepare mix
¾ cup whipping cream
1½ cup semisweet chocolate chips

*Refrigerate candy to make chopping easier.*

1. Preheat oven to 350°F. Line 60 mini (1¾-inch) muffin cups with paper baking cups. Finely chop peanut butter cups; refrigerate candy while preparing batter.

2. Prepare cake mix according to package directions; stir in 1 cup chopped candy. Spoon batter into prepared muffin cups, filling two-thirds full.

3. Bake 9 minutes or until toothpick inserted into centers comes out clean. Cool cupcakes in pans 5 minutes. Remove from pans; cool completely on wire racks.

4. Meanwhile, place cream in small saucepan. Bring to a boil over medium heat. Place chocolate chips in medium heatproof bowl; pour cream over chips. Let stand 5 minutes; stir until blended and smooth. Glaze will thicken as it cools. (Refrigerate glaze to thicken more quickly.)

5. Dip tops of cooled cupcakes in chocolate glaze; sprinkle with remaining chopped candy.                    *Makes 60 mini cupcakes*

# hot fudge sundae cake

1 package DUNCAN HINES® Moist Deluxe® Dark Chocolate Fudge
  Cake Mix
½ gallon brick vanilla ice cream

Fudge Sauce
  1 can (12 ounces) evaporated milk
1¼ cups sugar
  4 squares (1 ounce each) unsweetened chocolate
  ¼ cup (½ stick) butter or margarine
1½ teaspoons vanilla extract
  ¼ teaspoon salt
  Whipped cream and maraschino cherries for garnish

1. Preheat oven to 350°F. Grease and flour 13×9×2-inch pan. Prepare, bake and cool cake following package directions.

2. Remove cake from pan. Split cake in half horizontally. Place bottom layer back in pan. Cut ice cream into even slices and place evenly over bottom cake layer (use all the ice cream). Place remaining cake layer over ice cream. Cover and freeze.

3. For fudge sauce, combine evaporated milk and sugar in medium saucepan. Cook, stirring constantly, over medium heat until mixture comes to a rolling boil. Boil and stir for 1 minute. Add unsweetened chocolate and stir until melted. Beat over medium heat until smooth. Remove from heat. Stir in butter, vanilla extract and salt.

4. Cut cake into squares. For each serving, place cake square on plate; spoon hot fudge sauce on top. Garnish with whipped cream and maraschino cherry.                    *Makes 12 to 16 servings*

Tip: Fudge sauce may be prepared ahead and refrigerated in tightly sealed jar. Reheat when ready to serve.

# polka dot cake

1 package (about 18 ounces) chocolate cake mix, plus ingredients to prepare mix

¾ cup white chocolate chips

2 bars (3½ ounces each) good-quality bittersweet or semisweet chocolate, broken into small pieces

¼ cup (½ stick) butter, cut into small chunks

¼ cup whipping cream

1 tablespoon powdered sugar

Dash salt

¼ cup small chocolate nonpareil candies

1. Preheat oven to 350°F. Generously spray 12-cup bundt pan with nonstick cooking spray.

2. Prepare cake mix according to package directions. Pour batter into prepared pan; sprinkle with chocolate chips.

3. Bake 40 minutes or until toothpick inserted near center comes out clean. Cool cake in pan 30 minutes. Invert onto wire rack; cool completely. Place sheet of waxed paper under wire rack.

4. Combine chocolate pieces, butter, cream, powdered sugar and salt in small heavy saucepan. Heat over low heat, stirring constantly, just until butter and chocolate melt. Mixture should be tepid, not hot. Immediately spoon chocolate glaze over cake, spreading to cover side as well as top. Scoop up any glaze from waxed paper and spoon over cake.

5. Arrange nonpareil candies over glaze. Let glaze set about 2 hours at room temperature. Do not refrigerate. *Makes 16 servings*

# devil's food pancakes

1 package (about 18 ounces) devil's food cake mix
2 cups milk
2 eggs
½ cup mini chocolate chips
  Powdered sugar
  Strawberry Glaze (recipe follows, optional)

**1.** Whisk cake mix, milk and eggs in large bowl until well blended. Stir in chocolate chips.

**2.** Heat griddle or large nonstick skillet over medium-low to medium heat (350°F*). Pour ¼ cup batter onto griddle for each pancake. Cook 3 to 4 minutes or until edges appear dry; turn and cook 2 to 3 minutes. Repeat with remaining batter.

**3.** Sprinkle with powdered sugar and serve with Strawberry Glaze, if desired.                    *Makes about 22 (4-inch) pancakes*

*\*Do not cook pancakes at a higher temperature as they burn easily.*

Strawberry Glaze: **Combine 1 cup chopped fresh strawberries and ⅓ cup strawberry preserves in medium bowl.**

Note: **These pancakes freeze well. Freeze four pancakes in one resealable sandwich bag. Reheat in the microwave.**

# double chocolate chip snack cake

1 package (about 18 ounces) devil's food cake mix with pudding
    in the mix, divided
2 eggs
½ cup water
¼ cup vegetable oil
½ teaspoon cinnamon
1 cup semisweet chocolate chips, divided
¼ cup packed brown sugar
2 tablespoons butter, melted
¾ cup white chocolate chips

1. Preheat oven to 350°F. Grease 9-inch round cake pan.

2. Reserve ¾ cup cake mix. Beat remaining cake mix, eggs, water, oil and cinnamon in large bowl with electric mixer at medium speed 2 minutes. Remove ½ cup batter; reserve for another use.* Spread remaining batter in prepared pan; sprinkle with ½ cup semisweet chocolate chips.

3. Combine reserved cake mix and brown sugar in medium bowl. Stir in butter and remaining ½ cup semisweet chocolate chips; mix well. Sprinkle mixture over batter in pan.

4. Bake 35 to 40 minutes or until toothpick inserted into center comes out clean and cake springs back when lightly touched. Cool cake in pan 10 minutes. Remove from pan; cool completely on wire rack.

5. Place white chocolate chips in resealable food storage bag; seal bag. Microwave on HIGH 10 seconds and knead bag gently. Repeat until chips are melted. Cut off ¼ inch from corner of bag; drizzle chocolate over cake. Let glaze set before cutting cake into wedges.    *Makes 8 to 10 servings*

*If desired, extra batter can be used for cupcakes: Pour batter into two foil baking cups placed on baking sheet; bake at 350°F 20 to 25 minutes or until toothpick inserted into centers comes out clean.*

# chocolate dream torte

1 package DUNCAN HINES® Moist Deluxe® Dark Chocolate Fudge
  Cake Mix
1 (6-ounce) package semisweet chocolate chips, melted
1 (8-ounce) container frozen non-dairy whipped topping, thawed
1 container DUNCAN HINES® Creamy Home-Style Milk Chocolate
  Frosting
3 tablespoons finely chopped dry roasted pistachios

1. Preheat oven to 350°F. Grease and flour two 9-inch round cake pans.

2. Prepare, bake and cool cake as directed on package for basic recipe.

3. For chocolate hearts garnish, spread melted chocolate to ⅛-inch thickness on waxed paper-lined baking sheet. Cut shapes with heart cookie cutter when chocolate begins to set. Refrigerate until firm. Push out heart shapes. Set aside.

4. To assemble, split each cake layer in half horizontally. Place one split cake layer on serving plate. Spread one third of whipped topping on top. Repeat with remaining layers and whipped topping, leaving top plain. Frost side and top with frosting. Sprinkle pistachios on top. Position chocolate hearts by pushing points down into cake. Refrigerate until ready to serve.

*Makes 12 to 16 servings*

Chocolate Strawberry Dream Torte: Omit semisweet chocolate chips and chopped pistachios. Proceed as directed through step 2. Fold 1½ cups chopped fresh strawberries into whipped topping in large bowl. Assemble as directed, filling torte with strawberry mixture and frosting with Milk Chocolate frosting. Garnish cake with strawberry fans and mint leaves, if desired.

# chocolate crispy treat cake

1 package (about 18 ounces) chocolate fudge cake mix, plus
    ingredients to prepare mix
1 cup semisweet chocolate chips
¼ cup light corn syrup
¼ cup (½ stick) butter
½ cup powdered sugar
2 cups crisp rice cereal
4 cups mini marshmallows (half of 10½-ounce package)

1. Preheat oven to 350°F. Grease bottom only of 13×9-inch pan.

2. Prepare cake mix according to package directions; pour into prepared pan. Bake 28 minutes or until cake is almost done.

3. Meanwhile, heat chocolate chips, corn syrup and butter in medium saucepan over low heat, stirring frequently, until chocolate and butter are melted. Remove from heat; stir in powdered sugar. Gently stir in cereal until well blended.

4. Remove cake from oven; sprinkle marshmallows over top of cake in single layer. Return cake to oven; bake 2 to 3 minutes longer until marshmallows puff up slightly.

5. Spread chocolate cereal mixture over marshmallows. Let cake stand until set.                                    *Makes 24 servings*

Note: This cake is best within a day or two of baking; after two days the cereal becomes soggy.

# chocolate hazelnut cookies

½ cup chopped pecans
1 package (8 ounces) cream cheese, softened
½ cup (1 stick) butter, softened
1 egg
1 package (about 18 ounces) devil's food cake mix
1 jar (12 ounces) chocolate hazelnut spread
¼ cup powdered sugar

1. Preheat oven 350°F. Place pecans in small resealable food storage bag. Finely crush pecans with meat mallet or rolling pin. Place pecans in small skillet over medium high heat; toast 1½ minutes or until browned, stirring constantly. Remove from heat and set aside.

2. Beat cream cheese and butter in medium bowl with electric mixer at low speed 30 seconds or until smooth. Add egg; beat at medium speed until well blended. Add cake mix; beat at low speed 2 minutes until mixture is smooth and resembles thick cookie dough. Stir in pecans.

3. Shape dough into 1-inch balls; spray palms lightly with cooking spray, if necessary, to make handling easier. Place 1 inch apart on ungreased cookie sheets.

4. Bake 8 minutes. (Cookies will appear underbaked.) Cool cookies on cookie sheets 5 minutes. Remove to wire racks to cool completely.

5. Spoon 1 teaspoon chocolate hazelnut spread over each cookie; sprinkle with powdered sugar.                    *Makes 4 dozen cookies*

# fudgy mocha cupcakes with chocolate coffee ganache

1 package (about 18 ounces) devil's food cake mix *without* pudding in the mix

1 package (4-serving size) chocolate fudge instant pudding and pie filling mix

1⅓ cups strongly brewed coffee, cooled to room temperature

3 eggs

½ cup vegetable oil

6 ounces semisweet chocolate, finely chopped

½ cup whipping cream

2 teaspoons instant coffee granules

½ cup prepared white frosting

1. Preheat oven to 350°F. Line 18 standard (2½-inch) muffin cups with paper baking cups.

2. Beat cake mix, pudding mix, coffee, eggs and oil in large bowl with electric mixer at medium speed 2 minutes or until well blended. Spoon batter into prepared muffin cups, filling two-thirds full.

3. Bake 22 to 24 minutes or until toothpick inserted into centers comes out clean. Cool cupcakes in pans 10 minutes. Remove from pans; cool completely on wire racks.

4. For ganache, place chocolate in small bowl. Heat cream and instant coffee in small saucepan over medium-low heat until bubbles appear around edge of pan. Pour cream over chocolate; let stand about 2 minutes. Stir until mixture is smooth and shiny. Allow ganache to cool completely. (It will be slightly runny.)

5. Dip tops of cupcakes into ganache; smooth surface.

6. Place frosting in pastry bag fitted with small round writing tip. Pipe desired letters onto cupcakes. *Makes 18 cupcakes*

# chocolate petits fours

1 package DUNCAN HINES® Moist Deluxe® Dark Chocolate Fudge
    Cake Mix
1 package (7 ounces) pure almond paste
½ cup seedless red raspberry jam
3 cups semisweet chocolate chips
½ cup vegetable shortening plus additional for greasing

1. Preheat oven to 350°F. Grease and flour 13×9×2-inch pan.

2. Prepare, bake and cool cake following package directions for basic
recipe. Remove from pan. Cover and store overnight (see Tip on page 312).
Level top of cake. Trim ¼-inch strip of cake from all sides. (Be careful to
make straight cuts.) Cut cake into small squares, rectangles or triangles
with serrated knife. Cut round and heart shapes with 1½- to 2-inch cookie
cutters. Split each individual cake horizontally into two layers.

3. For filling, cut almond paste in half. Roll half the paste between two
sheets of waxed paper to ⅛-inch thickness. Cut into same shapes as
individual cakes. Repeat with second half of paste. Warm jam in small
saucepan over low heat until thin. Remove top of one cake. Spread
¼ to ½ teaspoon jam on inside of each cut surface. Place one almond
paste cutout on bottom layer. Top with second half of cake, jam side
down. Repeat with remaining cakes.

4. For glaze, place chocolate chips and ½ cup shortening in 4-cup glass
measuring cup. Microwave at MEDIUM (50% power) for 2 minutes; stir.
Microwave for 2 minutes longer at MEDIUM; stir until smooth. Place
3 assembled cakes on cooling rack over bowl. Spoon chocolate glaze
over each cake until top and sides are completely covered. Remove to
waxed paper when glaze has stopped dripping. Repeat process until all
cakes are covered. (Return chocolate glaze in bowl to glass measuring
cup as needed; microwave at MEDIUM for 30 to 60 seconds to thin.)

continued on page 312

5. Place remaining chocolate glaze in resealable plastic bag; seal. Place bag in bowl of hot water for several minutes. Dry with paper towel. Knead until chocolate is smooth. Snip pinpoint hole in bottom corner of bag. Drizzle or decorate top of each petit four. Let stand until chocolate is set. Store in single layer in airtight containers.     *Makes 24 to 32 servings*

Tip: To make cutting the cake into shapes easier, bake the cake one day before assembling.

# chocolate peanut butter candy bars

1 package (about 18 ounces) devil's food or dark chocolate cake mix *without* pudding in the mix
1 can (5 ounces) evaporated milk
⅓ cup butter, melted
½ cup dry-roasted peanuts
4 packages (1½ ounces each) chocolate peanut butter cups, coarsely chopped

1. Preheat oven to 350°F. Lightly grease 13×9-inch baking pan.

2. Beat cake mix, evaporated milk and butter in large bowl with electric mixer at medium speed until well blended. (Dough will be stiff.) Spread two thirds of dough in prepared pan. Sprinkle with peanuts.

3. Bake 10 minutes; remove from oven and sprinkle with chopped candy.

4. Drop remaining one third of dough by large spoonfuls over candy. Bake 15 to 20 minutes or until set. Cool completely in pan on wire rack.

*Makes 2 dozen bars*

# chocolate cream torte

1 package DUNCAN HINES® Moist Deluxe® Devil's Food Cake Mix
1 package (8 ounces) cream cheese, softened
½ cup sugar
1 teaspoon vanilla extract
1 cup finely chopped pecans
1 cup whipping cream, chilled
  Strawberry halves for garnish
  Mint leaves for garnish

1. Preheat oven to 350°F. Grease and flour two 8- or 9-inch round cake pans.

2. Prepare, bake and cool cake following package directions for basic recipe. Chill layers for ease in splitting.

3. Place cream cheese, sugar and vanilla extract in small bowl. Beat at low speed with electric mixer until smooth. Add pecans; stir until blended. Set aside. Beat whipping cream in small bowl until stiff peaks form. Fold whipped cream into cream cheese mixture.

4. To assemble, split each cake layer in half horizontally (see Tip). Place one cake layer on serving plate. Spread top with one fourth of filling. Repeat with remaining layers and filling. Garnish with strawberry halves and mint leaves, if desired. Refrigerate until ready to serve.

*Makes 12 to 16 servings*

Tip: To split layers evenly, measure cake with ruler. Divide into 2 equal layers. Mark with toothpicks. Cut through layers with serrated knife, using toothpicks as guide.

# dark chocolate lava cakes

1½ cups cold milk
1 package (4-serving size) chocolate instant pudding and
  pie filling mix
1 package (about 18 ounces) dark chocolate cake mix
1 cup buttermilk
2 eggs
3 egg yolks
¼ cup vegetable oil
2 tablespoons water
1 tablespoon butter, melted
¼ cup granulated sugar
  Sifted powdered sugar

**1.** Combine milk and pudding mix in medium bowl; whisk until smooth. Place plastic wrap on surface of pudding; refrigerate.

**2.** Combine cake mix, buttermilk, eggs, egg yolks, oil and water in large bowl; stir with spatula until almost smooth (some lumps will remain). *Do not use electric mixer.* Cover batter and refrigerate 1 hour.

**3.** Preheat oven to 400°F. Brush melted butter inside 14 (5-ounce) custard cups. Sprinkle evenly with granulated sugar. Place cups on rimmed baking sheet.

**4.** Place 2 tablespoons batter in each prepared custard cup. Bake 10 to 12 minutes (batter will not cook through completely). Remove cups from oven; place 1 heaping tablespoon pudding in center of each cup and top with 2 tablespoons batter.

**5.** Bake 14 to 16 minutes or until toothpick inserted into top layer of cakes comes out clean. Remove cups to wire racks; cool 7 to 10 minutes. Invert cakes onto plates. Sprinkle with powdered sugar; serve immediately.

*Makes 14 cakes*

# chocolate peanut butter birthday cake

1 package (about 18 ounces) devil's food cake mix, plus ingredients
    to prepare mix
1 package (about 11 ounces) peanut butter and chocolate chips
1 container (16 ounces) milk chocolate frosting
    Assorted fruit roll-ups
    Candles or thin pretzel sticks

1. Preheat oven to 350°F. Grease and flour two 8-inch round cake pans.

2. Prepare cake mix according to package directions; stir in ⅓ cup peanut butter and chocolate chips. Pour batter into prepared pans. Bake 30 minutes or until toothpick inserted into centers comes out clean. Cool cake layers in pans 10 minutes. Remove from pans; cool completely on wire racks.

3. Place one cake layer on serving plate; spread with ½ cup frosting. Top with second cake layer; frost top and side of cake with remaining frosting. Gently press remaining peanut butter and chocolate chips onto side of cake and around top edge of cake.

4. To make decorative flags, cut desired amount of triangles out of fruit roll-ups. Make two ½- to ¾-inch horizontal cuts along short side of one triangle. Weave one candle in and out of cuts. Repeat with remaining triangles and candles. Arrange flags on cake.          *Makes 12 servings*

# layered chocolate torte

1 package (about 16 ounces) pound cake mix, plus ingredients
   to prepare mix
6 ounces bittersweet chocolate, broken into pieces
1 container (8 ounces) frozen whipped topping, thawed
¼ cup plus 2 tablespoons sour cream
   Chocolate curls (optional)

**1.** Preheat oven to 400°F. Line 15×10-inch jelly-roll pan with parchment paper. Prepare cake mix according to package directions; pour batter into pan and spread evenly.

**2.** Bake 12 to 14 minutes or until toothpick inserted into center comes out clean. Cool cake in pan 10 minutes. Remove from pan (lift cake and parchment up together to easily slide cake out of pan); cool completely on wire rack or countertop.

**3.** Place chocolate in medium microwavable bowl. Microwave on HIGH 1½ minutes or until melted, stirring after 1 minute. Cool slightly; fold in whipped topping and sour cream until well blended.

**4.** Place cake on cutting board; cut crosswise into 4 equal pieces. Place one cake layer on serving plate; spread with chocolate mixture. Repeat with second and third cake layers and chocolate mixture. Top with fourth cake layer; spread remaining chocolate mixture over top and sides of cake. Refrigerate 1 hour before serving. Garnish with chocolate curls.

*Makes about 12 servings*

# rocky road cake

1 cup chopped walnuts or pecans or dry roasted peanuts
1 package (about 18 ounces) devil's food cake mix
1⅓ cups water
3 eggs
½ cup vegetable oil
2 teaspoons instant coffee granules (optional)
4 cups mini marshmallows
1 jar (16 ounces) hot fudge topping

1. Preheat oven to 350°F. Grease bottom only of 13×9-inch baking pan.

2. Toast walnuts in medium skillet over medium-high heat 3 to 4 minutes or until just beginning to brown, stirring frequently. Remove from heat; set aside.

3. Beat cake mix, water, eggs, oil and instant coffee, if desired, in large bowl with electric mixer at low speed 1 minute or until well blended. Pour batter into prepared pan.

4. Bake 33 minutes or until toothpick inserted into center comes out almost clean. Remove cake to wire rack; immediately sprinkle with marshmallows, then walnuts. Let stand 15 minutes.

5. Heat hot fudge topping in microwave according to package directions. Drizzle evenly over cake. Cool completely before serving.

*Makes 16 servings*

# Holiday
*Treats*

# chocolate sweetheart cupcakes

1 package (about 18 ounces) dark chocolate cake mix, plus
    ingredients to prepare mix
1 container (16 ounces) vanilla frosting
3 tablespoons seedless raspberry jam
    Powdered sugar (optional)

1. Preheat oven to 350°F. Line 24 standard (2½-inch) muffin cups with paper baking cups.

2. Prepare cake mix according to package directions. Spoon batter into prepared muffin cups, filling two-thirds full.

3. Bake 18 minutes or until toothpick inserted into centers comes out clean. Cool cupcakes in pans 10 minutes. Remove from pans; cool completely on wire racks.

4. Blend frosting and jam in medium bowl until smooth. Cut off rounded tops of cupcakes with serrated knife. Cut out heart shape from each cupcake top with mini cookie cutter.

5. Spread frosting mixture generously over cupcake bottoms, mounding slightly in center. Replace cupcake tops, pressing gently to fill cutout hearts with frosting mixture. Sprinkle with powdered sugar, if desired.

*Makes 24 cupcakes*

# i think you're "marbleous" cupcakes

        1 package (about 18 ounces) cake mix, any flavor, with pudding
            in the mix
    1¼ cups water
        3 eggs
    ¼ cup vegetable oil
        1 container (16 ounces) vanilla frosting
        1 tube red decorating icing

1. Preheat oven to 350°F. Line 24 standard (2½-inch) muffin cups with paper baking cups or spray with nonstick cooking spray.

2. Beat cake mix, water, eggs and oil in large bowl with electric mixer at low speed 30 seconds. Beat at medium speed 2 minutes or until well blended. Spoon batter into prepared muffin cups, filling two-thirds full.

3. Bake 20 to 25 minutes or until toothpick inserted into centers comes out clean. Cool cupcakes in pans 20 minutes. Remove from pans; cool completely on wire racks.

4. Spread 1½ to 2 tablespoons frosting over each cupcake. Fit round decorating tip onto tube of icing. Squeeze 5 dots of icing over each cupcake. Swirl toothpick through icing and frosting in continuous motion to make marbleized pattern or heart shapes.          *Makes 24 cupcakes*

# pretty-in-pink peppermint cupcakes

      1 package (about 18 ounces) white cake mix
$1\frac{1}{3}$ cups water
      3 egg whites
      2 tablespoons vegetable oil or melted butter
      $\frac{1}{2}$ teaspoon peppermint extract
      3 to 4 drops red liquid food coloring *or* $\frac{1}{4}$ teaspoon red gel
            food coloring
      1 container (16 ounces) vanilla frosting
      $\frac{1}{2}$ cup crushed peppermint candies (about 16 candies)

1. Preheat oven to 350°F. Line 30 standard (2½-inch) muffin cups with paper baking cups.

2. Beat cake mix, water, egg whites, oil, peppermint extract and food coloring in large bowl with electric mixer at low speed 30 seconds. Beat at medium speed 2 minutes. Spoon batter into prepared muffin cups, filling three-fourths full.

3. Bake 20 to 22 minutes or until toothpick inserted into centers comes out clean. Cool cupcakes in pans 10 minutes. Remove from pans; cool completely on wire racks. (At this point, cupcakes may be frozen up to 3 months. Thaw at room temperature before frosting.)

4. Spread frosting over cooled cupcakes; sprinkle with crushed candies. Store at room temperature up to 24 hours or cover and refrigerate up to 3 days before serving.                    *Makes 30 cupcakes*

# angelic cupcakes

 1 package (about 16 ounces) angel food cake mix
1¼ cups cold water
 ¼ teaspoon peppermint extract (optional)
    Red food coloring
4½ cups thawed frozen whipped topping

1. Preheat oven to 375°F. Line 36 standard (2½-inch) muffin cups with paper baking cups.

2. Beat cake mix, water and peppermint extract, if desired, in large bowl with electric mixer at low speed 2 minutes.

3. Pour half of batter into medium bowl; fold in 9 drops red food coloring. Alternate spoonfuls of white and pink batter in each prepared muffin cup, filling three-fourths full.

4. Bake 11 minutes or until cupcakes are golden brown with deep cracks on top. Remove from pans; cool completely on wire racks.

5. Divide whipped topping between two small bowls. Add 2 drops red food coloring to one bowl of whipped topping; stir gently until blended. Frost cupcakes with pink and white whipped topping. Refrigerate leftovers.

*Makes 36 cupcakes*

# green's lucky cake

1 package (18.25 ounces) any flavor cake mix, plus ingredients
   to prepare mix
1/2 teaspoon water
2 to 3 drops green food coloring
1/2 cup sweetened shredded coconut
6 tablespoons butter, softened
3¾ cups powdered sugar, divided
3 to 4 tablespoons milk
1/2 teaspoon vanilla extract
   Blue food coloring
1 cup "M&M's"® Chocolate Mini Baking Bits

Prepare and bake cake as directed on package for 13×9-inch cake. Cool cake completely on wire rack. In small bowl combine water and food coloring. Add coconut and stir until evenly tinted; set aside. In large bowl cream butter until light. Add 2 cups powdered sugar; beat until fluffy. Blend in 3 tablespoons milk and vanilla. Beat in remaining 1¾ cups powdered sugar until frosting is smooth. Add additional milk, 1 teaspoon at a time, if necessary to make frosting spreadable. Tint frosting desired shade of blue. Frost cake and decorate with tinted coconut and "M&M's"® Chocolate Mini Baking Bits as shown in photo.            *Makes 16 to 20 servings*

# kelly green mini bundt cakes

2 tablespoons butter, melted
1 package (about 18 ounces) white cake mix, plus ingredients
    to prepare mix
  Green food coloring
1 container (16 ounces) white frosting
  Green decorating sugar

1. Preheat oven to 350°F. Brush 12 mini (1-cup) bundt pan cups with butter.

2. Prepare cake mix according to package directions. Add food coloring to batter, one drop at a time, until desired shade of green is reached. Fill prepared bundt pan cups half full.

3. Bake 20 minutes or until toothpick inserted near centers comes out clean. Cool cakes in pans 5 minutes. Carefully place wire rack on top of each pan; invert pans. Lightly tap bottom of pans to help release cakes. Cool completely on wire racks.

4. Place frosting in small microwavable bowl. Add food coloring, one drop at a time, until desired shade of green is reached. Microwave on LOW (30%) for 30 seconds or until pourable but not melted. Spoon frosting over tops of cakes. Sprinkle with green sugar. *Makes 12 mini cakes*

# leprechaun cupcakes

1 package (about 18 ounces) yellow or white cake mix,
   plus ingredients to prepare mix
1 container (16 ounces) vanilla frosting
   Green, orange and red gumdrops, black decorating gel
   and small candies

1. Preheat oven to 350°F. Line 24 standard (2½-inch) muffin cups with paper baking cups.

2. Prepare cake mix according to package directions. Spoon batter into prepared muffin cups, filling two-thirds full.

3. Bake 15 to 20 minutes or until toothpick inserted into centers comes out clean. Cool cupcakes in pans 10 minutes. Remove from pans; cool completely on wire racks. Frost cupcakes with vanilla frosting.

4. Roll out green gumdrops on generously sugared surface. Cut out pieces to resemble hats. Pipe gel onto hats for hatbands; place candies on hatbands for buckles. Place hats on cupcakes. Roll out orange gumdrops on generously sugared surface. Cut out pieces to resemble sideburns and beards; place on cupcakes. Roll out red gumdrops on generously sugared surface. Cut out small pieces to resemble mouths; place on cupcakes. Place candies on cupcakes for eyes.    *Makes 24 cupcakes*

# lucky shamrock cake

1 package (about 18 ounces) white cake mix, plus ingredients
to prepare mix
1 container (16 ounces) white frosting
2 tubes green decorating icing
Irish-themed candy decorations

1. Prepare and bake cake mix according to package directions for two
9-inch round cake layers. Cool completely before frosting.

2. Place one cake layer on serving plate; spread with frosting. Top with
second cake layer; frost top and side of cake.

3. Pipe green icing around base of cake to resemble blades of grass.
Decorate with candy decorations as desired.           *Makes 12 servings*

# luck o' the irish cupcakes

1 package (about 18 ounces) cake mix, any flavor, plus ingredients
    to prepare mix
1 container (16 ounces) white frosting
1 tube green decorating icing
    Green and orange sprinkles, decors and colored sugars

1. Preheat oven to 350°F. Line 24 standard (2½-inch) muffin cups with paper baking cups.

2. Prepare cake mix according to package directions. Spoon batter into prepared muffin cups, filling two-thirds full.

3. Bake 15 to 20 minutes or until toothpick inserted into centers comes out clean. Cool cupcakes in pans 10 minutes. Remove from pans; cool completely on wire racks.

4. Frost cupcakes. Use icing to pipe Irish words or shamrock designs onto cupcakes. Decorate as desired. *Makes 24 cupcakes*

# easy easter cupcakes

1 package (about 18 ounces) yellow cake mix, plus ingredients to prepare mix
1 container (16 ounces) vanilla frosting
  Green food coloring
24 sugar-coated colored marshmallow chicks and/or rabbits
  Assorted white candies

1. Preheat oven to 350°F. Line 24 standard (2½-inch) muffin cups with paper baking cups.

2. Prepare and bake cake mix according to package directions for cupcakes. Cool cupcakes in pans 10 minutes. Remove from pans; cool completely on wire racks.

3. Blend food coloring and frosting in medium bowl until desired shade of green is reached. Frost tops of cupcakes.

4. Trim marshmallow animals with scissors or knife to fit on cupcakes. Arrange marshmallows on frosting; decorate edges of cupcakes with candies.                                           *Makes 24 cupcakes*

# liberty's torches

26 flat-bottomed ice cream cones
1 package (about 18 ounces) cake mix, any flavor, plus ingredients to prepare mix
1 container (16 ounces) white frosting
   Yellow food coloring
26 red, yellow and orange fruit roll-ups

1. Preheat oven to 350°F. Stand 24 ice cream cones in 13×9-inch pan and remaining 2 cones in muffin cups or small loaf pan. (Or, place all cones in muffin cups.)

2. Prepare cake mix according to package directions. Fill each cone with 2½ tablespoons batter (filling to within about ¼ inch of top of cone base).

3. Bake 30 minutes or until cake tops spring back when lightly touched and toothpick inserted into centers comes out clean. Remove cones to wire racks; cool completely.

4. Blend frosting and food coloring in medium bowl until desired shade of yellow is reached. Frost cupcakes. Cut flames from fruit roll-ups using kitchen shears or sharp knife. Fold or roll flames to stand upright; arrange on cupcakes before frosting sets.

*Makes 26 cupcakes*

# spider cupcakes

1 package (about 18 ounces) yellow or white cake mix
1 cup solid-pack pumpkin
¾ cup water
3 eggs
2 tablespoons vegetable oil
1 teaspoon ground cinnamon
1 teaspoon pumpkin pie spice*
1 container (16 ounces) vanilla, cream cheese or caramel frosting
    Orange food coloring
4 squares (1 ounce each) semisweet chocolate
48 black gumdrops

*Or substitute ½ teaspoon ground cinnamon, ¼ teaspoon ground ginger and ⅛ teaspoon each ground allspice and ground nutmeg for the pumpkin pie spice.*

1. Preheat oven to 350°F. Line 24 standard (2½-inch) muffin cups with paper baking cups or spray with nonstick cooking spray.

2. Beat cake mix, pumpkin, water, eggs, oil, cinnamon and pumpkin pie spice in large bowl with electric mixer at medium speed 3 minutes or until well blended. Spoon ¼ cup batter into each muffin cup. Bake 20 minutes or until toothpick inserted into centers comes out clean. Cool cupcakes in pans 10 minutes. Remove from pans; cool completely on wire racks.

3. Blend frosting and food coloring in medium bowl until desired shade of orange is reached. Frost cupcakes.

4. Place chocolate in small resealable food storage bag. Microwave on MEDIUM (50%) 40 seconds. Knead bag; microwave 30 seconds to 1 minute or until chocolate is melted and smooth. Cut off tiny corner of bag. Drizzle chocolate in four or five concentric circles over top of cupcakes. Immediately draw 6 to 8 lines at regular intervals from center to edges of cupcakes with toothpick or knife to create web.

*continued on page 348*

5. For spiders, place one gumdrop in center of web. Roll out another gumdrop with rolling pin on generously sugared surface. Slice thinly and roll into "legs." Arrange legs around gumdrop to form spiders.

*Makes 24 cupcakes*

# deadly diamonds

1 package (9 ounces) devil's food cake mix, plus ingredients
    to prepare mix
1 cup marshmallow creme
¼ cup red currant jelly

1. Prepare and bake cake mix according to package directions in 9-inch square baking pan. Cool cake in pan 15 minutes. Remove from pan; cool completely on wire rack.

2. Cut cake into 4 strips. Trim edges; cut each strip on diagonal to form 4 diamonds (total of 16 diamonds).

3. Just before serving, spread 1 tablespoon marshmallow creme over each diamond. Place jelly in small microwavable bowl; microwave on LOW (30%) 20 to 30 seconds. Stir until melted. Drizzle about ½ teaspoon jelly over each diamond; swirl into marshmallow surface to create dripping effect. Serve immediately.

*Makes 16 servings*

# squished and squirmy sandwiches

1 package (9 ounces) vanilla confetti cake mix
2 eggs
$\frac{1}{3}$ cup vegetable oil
2 pints vanilla ice cream
32 gummy worms

1. Preheat oven to 375°F.

2. Mix cake mix, eggs and oil in large bowl with spoon until well moistened. Shape dough into 32 (1$\frac{1}{4}$-inch) balls. Place 2 inches apart on ungreased cookie sheets. Gently flatten dough to $\frac{1}{4}$-inch thickness.

3. Bake 6 to 8 minutes or until edges are light golden brown. Cool cookies on cookie sheets 1 minute; remove to wire racks to cool completely.

4. Working quickly, place 2 tablespoons ice cream on flat side of one cookie and top with gummy worm, allowing worm to stick out as much as possible. Top with 2 tablespoons ice cream and another worm. Top with another cookie, flat side down, pressing down to flatten slightly. Wrap in foil and freeze. Repeat with remaining cookies, ice cream and gummy worms.                          *Makes 16 sandwiches*

When shaping the dough, try to create cookies that are uniform in size and shape so they finish baking at the same time. For even baking and browning of cookies, bake them in the center of the oven. If the heat distribution in your oven is uneven, turn the cookie sheet halfway through the baking time.

# scaredy cat cake

1 package (about 18 ounces) devil's food cake mix, plus ingredients
   to prepare mix
1 container (16 ounces) dark chocolate fudge frosting
4 individual square chocolate snack cakes
1 large orange or pink gumdrop
   Granulated sugar
   Black decorating gel
   Black string licorice, cut into $3\frac{1}{2}$- to 4-inch lengths
2 large yellow gumdrops

1. Prepare and bake cake mix according to package directions for two 8-inch round cake layers. Cool cake layers in pans 15 minutes. Remove from pans; cool completely on wire racks.

2. Place one cake layer on serving plate; spread with frosting. Top with second cake layer; frost top and side of cake.

3. Cut snack cakes in half diagonally. Frost tops of all snack cake triangles. Make 2 stacks of 4 triangles each. Place at top of round cake for ears; frost to blend in with round cake. Use back of spoon to pull frosting on side of cake out into points to resemble fur.

4. Roll out orange gumdrop with rolling pin on generously sugared surface. Cut out large triangle; place in center of cake for nose. Use decorating gel to create mouth and licorice for whiskers.

5. Roll out yellow gumdrops with rolling pin on generously sugared surface. Cut out pointed ovals; place on cake for eyes. Pipe gel onto eyes.

*Makes 12 servings*

# boo hands cupcakes

1 package (about 18 ounces) cake mix, any flavor, plus ingredients to prepare mix
1 container (16 ounces) white frosting
36 large marshmallows
24 black jelly beans, halved
12 orange jelly beans, halved

1. Preheat oven to 350°F. Line 24 standard (2½-inch) muffin cups with paper baking cups or spray with nonstick cooking spray.

2. Prepare cake mix according to package directions. Spoon batter evenly into prepared muffin cups.

3. Bake 15 to 20 minutes or until toothpick inserted into centers comes out clean. Cool cupcakes in pans 15 minutes. Remove from pans; cool completely on wire racks.

4. Spread small amount of frosting on cupcakes. Cut 12 marshmallows in half crosswise; place one half on each cupcake. Frost cupcakes again, completely covering marshmallow half.

5. Roll each remaining marshmallow between hands to about 2½ inches in length. Cut in half and arrange on either side of cupcake to create hands; cover completely with frosting. Create faces using 2 black jelly bean halves for eyes and orange jelly bean half for nose.          *Makes 24 cupcakes*

# blue goo cupcakes

1 package (about 18 ounces) white cake mix, plus ingredients to prepare mix
Blue food coloring
1 package (6 ounces) blue gelatin
1⅓ cups boiling water
Blue decorating icing

1. Preheat oven to 350°F. Line 24 standard (2½-inch) muffin cups with paper baking cups.

2. Prepare cake mix according to package directions. Stir food coloring into batter until desired shade of blue is reached. Spoon batter into prepared muffin cups, filling two-thirds full.

3. Bake according to package directions. Cool cupcakes in pans 5 minutes. Remove from pans; cool completely on wire racks.

4. Meanwhile, combine gelatin and boiling water in small bowl. Stir 3 minutes or until gelatin is completely dissolved. Freeze mixture 40 minutes or until partially set, stirring often.

5. Pipe ring of blue icing around edge of each cupcake. Spoon 1 rounded tablespoon gelatin mixture into center. *Makes 24 cupcakes*

Tip: For a firm texture, or in extreme heat, chill cupcakes until ready to serve. For a runny "blob" consistency, serve at room temperature.

# ooze cupcakes

1 package (8 ounces) cream cheese, softened
½ cup powdered sugar
⅓ cup thawed frozen limeade concentrate
1 teaspoon vanilla
  Yellow and blue food coloring
1 package (about 18 ounces) chocolate cake mix, plus ingredients
    to prepare mix
1 container (16 ounces) vanilla frosting
  Orange sugar

1. Preheat oven to 350°F. Line 24 standard (2½-inch) muffin cups with paper baking cups or spray with nonstick cooking spray.

2. Beat cream cheese, powdered sugar, limeade concentrate and vanilla in large bowl with electric mixer at medium speed until well blended. Beat in yellow food coloring until desired shade of yellow is reached.

3. Prepare cake mix according to package directions, using 1 egg instead of 3. Spoon batter into prepared muffin cups, filling half full. Spoon 1 rounded teaspoon cream cheese mixture into center of each cup.

4. Bake 20 minutes or until toothpick inserted into centers comes out clean. Cool cupcakes in pans 10 minutes. Remove from pans; cool completely on wire racks.

5. Add 4 drops yellow food coloring and 2 drops blue food coloring to frosting; stir until well blended. Add additional food coloring, if necessary, until desired shade of green is reached. Frost cupcakes; sprinkle with orange sugar. *Makes 24 cupcakes*

# pumpkin cheesecake bars

1 (16-ounce) package pound cake mix

3 eggs, divided

2 tablespoons butter or margarine, melted

4 teaspoons pumpkin pie spice, divided

1 (8-ounce) package cream cheese, softened

1 (14-ounce) can **EAGLE BRAND**® Sweetened Condensed Milk
    (**NOT** evaporated milk)

1 (15-ounce) can pumpkin (2 cups)

½ teaspoon salt

1 cup chopped nuts

1. Preheat oven to 350°F. In large bowl, on low speed, combine cake mix, 1 egg, butter and 2 teaspoons pumpkin pie spice until crumbly. Press onto bottom of ungreased 15×10-inch jelly roll pan.

2. In large bowl, beat cream cheese until fluffy. Gradually beat in EAGLE BRAND® until smooth. Beat in remaining 2 eggs, pumpkin, remaining 2 teaspoons pumpkin pie spice and salt; mix well.

3. Pour into prepared crust; sprinkle with nuts.

4. Bake 30 to 35 minutes or until set. Cool. Chill; cut into bars. Store leftovers covered in refrigerator.                *Makes 4 dozen bars*

# snowman cupcakes

1 package (about 18 ounces) yellow or white cake mix,
    plus ingredients to prepare mix
2 containers (16 ounces each) vanilla frosting
4 cups shredded coconut
15 large marshmallows
15 miniature chocolate covered peanut butter cups
    Small red candies
    Pretzel sticks
    Green and red decorating gels

1. Preheat oven to 350°F. Grease 15 standard (2½-inch) muffin cups and 15 mini (1¾-inch) muffin cups.

2. Prepare cake mix according to package directions. Spoon batter into prepared muffin cups, filling two-thirds full.

3. Bake 10 to 15 minutes for mini cupcakes and 15 to 20 minutes for standard cupcakes or until golden and toothpick inserted into centers comes out clean. Cool cupcakes in pans 10 minutes. Remove from pans; cool completely on wire racks.

4. To assemble, frost bottoms and sides of large cupcakes; coat with coconut. Repeat with mini cupcakes. Attach mini cupcakes to large cupcakes with frosting to form snowman bodies. Attach marshmallows to mini cupcakes with frosting to form heads. Attach inverted peanut butter cups to marshmallows with frosting to form hats. Use pretzels for arms and red candies for buttons as shown in photo. Pipe faces with decorating gels. *Makes 15 snowmen*

# butter pecan sweet potato crunch

2 cans (15 ounces each) **PRINCELLA**® or **SUGARY SAM**®
   Cut Sweet Potatoes, drained and mashed
1 can (12 ounces) evaporated milk
1 cup sugar
3 eggs
1 tablespoon cinnamon
1 teaspoon vanilla
½ (18¼-ounce) package yellow cake mix (dry)
1 cup chopped pecans
½ cup (1 stick) butter or margarine, melted
   Whipped topping

Preheat oven to 350°F. In large bowl, combine first six ingredients. Pour sweet potato mixture into greased 13×9-inch baking pan. Sprinkle dry cake mix on top. Cover with chopped pecans. Drizzle melted butter or margarine on top of pecans. Bake for about 1 hour or until center is firm. Chill well. Cut into squares. Serve with whipped topping.

*Makes 15 to 20 servings*

# reindeer cupcakes

1 package (about 18 ounces) chocolate cake mix, plus ingredients to prepare mix

¼ cup (½ stick) butter, softened

4 cups powdered sugar

5 to 6 tablespoons brewed espresso

½ cup semisweet chocolate chips, melted

1 teaspoon vanilla

Dash salt

24 pretzel twists, broken in half

Assorted candies

1. Preheat oven to 350°F. Line 24 standard (2½-inch) muffin cups with paper baking cups.

2. Prepare cake mix according to package directions. Spoon batter into prepared muffin cups, filling two-thirds full.

3. Bake 15 to 20 minutes or until toothpick inserted into centers comes out clean. Cool cupcakes in pans 10 minutes. Remove from pans; cool completely on wire racks.

4. Beat butter in large bowl with electric mixer at medium speed until creamy. Gradually add powdered sugar and 4 tablespoons espresso; beat until smooth. Add melted chocolate, vanilla and salt; beat until well blended. Add remaining espresso, 1 tablespoon at a time, until frosting reaches desired spreading consistency.

5. Frost cupcakes. Decorate with broken pretzel pieces for antlers and assorted candies for faces.

*Makes 24 cupcakes*

# classic pumpkin roll

1¼ cups powdered sugar, divided
1 package (about 16 ounces) angel food cake mix
1¼ cups water
1 package (8 ounces) cream cheese, softened
1 container (8 ounces) whipped topping, thawed
½ cup solid-pack pumpkin
Cream Cheese Frosting (recipe follows)
½ cup chopped hazelnuts

1. Preheat oven to 350°F. Spray 17×12-inch jelly-roll pan with nonstick cooking spray. Line pan with waxed paper. Sprinkle clean towel with ½ cup powdered sugar; set aside.

2. Beat cake mix and water in large bowl according to package directions. Pour batter into prepared pan. Bake 17 minutes or until toothpick inserted into center comes out clean. Immediately invert cake onto prepared towel. Fold towel edge over cake edge and roll up cake and towel jelly-roll style into 12-inch-long roll. Place roll seam side down on wire rack to cool completely.

3. Beat cream cheese and remaining ¾ cup powdered sugar in large bowl with electric mixer 2 minutes or until fluffy. Fold in whipped topping and pumpkin; refrigerate until ready to use. Prepare Cream Cheese Frosting.

4. Slowly and carefully unroll cake onto serving plate, removing towel. Spread pumpkin filling evenly over cake. Re-roll cake; place roll seam side down on plate. Spread frosting over cake; sprinkle with hazelnuts. Cut 1 inch off each end of cake with serrated knife; discard scraps. Cover with plastic wrap; refrigerate 2 to 3 hours before serving.      *Makes 10 servings*

Cream Cheese Frosting: Beat 2 packages (8 ounces each) softened cream cheese and ½ cup (1 stick) softened butter in large bowl with electric mixer at medium-high speed 2 minutes or until well blended and fluffy. Add 2 cups powdered sugar, sifted, and 2 teaspoons vanilla; beat until well blended.

# cranberry chocolate cake

1 package (about 18 ounces) devil's food cake mix

1⅓ cups water

3 eggs

½ cup vegetable oil

1 can (16 ounces) whole berry cranberry sauce, divided

1 container (8 ounces) thawed frozen whipped topping

2 tablespoons cocoa powder

1 cup sliced almonds, toasted*

*To toast almonds, spread in single layer on baking sheet. Bake in preheated 350°F oven 7 to 9 minutes or until golden brown, stirring frequently.

1. Preheat oven to 350°F. Grease bottom only of 13×9-inch baking pan.

2. Prepare cake mix with water, eggs and oil according to package directions. Add half of cranberry sauce; beat until well blended. Pour batter into prepared pan. Bake 30 minutes or until toothpick inserted into center comes out clean. Cool completely in pan on wire rack.

3. Place whipped topping in medium bowl. Sift cocoa over whipped topping; fold mixture until well blended.

4. When cake has cooled, place remaining cranberry sauce in small microwavable bowl; microwave on HIGH 15 seconds or until softened. Spoon over cake; spread evenly using back of spoon. Top with whipped topping mixture. Cover with plastic wrap and refrigerate until ready to serve. Sprinkle with almonds just before serving.                    *Makes 20 servings*

# Acknowledgments

**The publisher would like to thank the companies listed below for the use of their recipes and photographs in this publication.**

Allens®

Dole Food Company, Inc.

Duncan Hines® and Moist Deluxe® are registered trademarks of Pinnacle Foods Corp.

EAGLE BRAND®

The Hershey Company

© Mars, Incorporated 2007

Nestlé USA

# METRIC CONVERSION CHART

## VOLUME MEASUREMENTS (dry)

1/8 teaspoon = 0.5 mL
1/4 teaspoon = 1 mL
1/2 teaspoon = 2 mL
3/4 teaspoon = 4 mL
1 teaspoon = 5 mL
1 tablespoon = 15 mL
2 tablespoons = 30 mL
1/4 cup = 60 mL
1/3 cup = 75 mL
1/2 cup = 125 mL
2/3 cup = 150 mL
3/4 cup = 175 mL
1 cup = 250 mL
2 cups = 1 pint = 500 mL
3 cups = 750 mL
4 cups = 1 quart = 1 L

## VOLUME MEASUREMENTS (fluid)

1 fluid ounce (2 tablespoons) = 30 mL
4 fluid ounces (1/2 cup) = 125 mL
8 fluid ounces (1 cup) = 250 mL
12 fluid ounces (1 1/2 cups) = 375 mL
16 fluid ounces (2 cups) = 500 mL

## WEIGHTS (mass)

1/2 ounce = 15 g
1 ounce = 30 g
3 ounces = 90 g
4 ounces = 120 g
8 ounces = 225 g
10 ounces = 285 g
12 ounces = 360 g
16 ounces = 1 pound = 450 g

## DIMENSIONS

1/16 inch = 2 mm
1/8 inch = 3 mm
1/4 inch = 6 mm
1/2 inch = 1.5 cm
3/4 inch = 2 cm
1 inch = 2.5 cm

## OVEN TEMPERATURES

250°F = 120°C
275°F = 140°C
300°F = 150°C
325°F = 160°C
350°F = 180°C
375°F = 190°C
400°F = 200°C
425°F = 220°C
450°F = 230°C

## BAKING PAN SIZES

| Utensil | Size in Inches/Quarts | Metric Volume | Size in Centimeters |
|---|---|---|---|
| Baking or Cake Pan (square or rectangular) | 8 × 8 × 2 | 2 L | 20 × 20 × 5 |
| | 9 × 9 × 2 | 2.5 L | 23 × 23 × 5 |
| | 12 × 8 × 2 | 3 L | 30 × 20 × 5 |
| | 13 × 9 × 2 | 3.5 L | 33 × 23 × 5 |
| Loaf Pan | 8 × 4 × 3 | 1.5 L | 20 × 10 × 7 |
| | 9 × 5 × 3 | 2 L | 23 × 13 × 7 |
| Round Layer Cake Pan | 8 × 1½ | 1.2 L | 20 × 4 |
| | 9 × 1½ | 1.5 L | 23 × 4 |
| Pie Plate | 8 × 1¼ | 750 mL | 20 × 3 |
| | 9 × 1¼ | 1 L | 23 × 3 |
| Baking Dish or Casserole | 1 quart | 1 L | — |
| | 1½ quart | 1.5 L | — |
| | 2 quart | 2 L | — |